The Unveiled Christos

David Spangler

DEDICATION

This book is lovingly dedicated
to the Christos within us each.

THE UNVEILED CHRISTOS

Copyright © 2025 David Spangler

David Spangler has asserted his right to be identified as the author of this work. All rights are reserved, including the right to reproduce this book, or portions thereof, in any form. Reviewers may quote brief passages. Artificial Intelligence (AI) use of this material is strictly prohibited.

Cover and Interior Design by Jeremy Berg

Published by Lorian Press LLC
Coloma, Michigan

ISBN: 978-1-939790-74-3

Spangler/David
The Unveiled Christos/David Spangler

First Edition: February 2025

Printed in the United States of America
and other countries

www.lorian.org

ACKNOWLEDGMENTS

The content of this book is taken from an online class that I offered through the Lorian Association in 2005. I want to acknowledge all the people who participated in this class. Your encouragement, questions, and contributions helped me give form and coherence to this material. I also want to thank Jeremy Berg both for his wonderful cover and for formatting the original transcript of this class into a more readable book format.

CONTENTS

Foreword by Lee Irwin	1
Introduction	7
Chapter One: Sacredness	9
Chapter Two: Thinking About Christ	21
Chapter Three: Redemption & The Christ Of History	29
Chapter Four: Jesus & The Christ Of Incarnation	51
Chapter Five: The Cosmic Christ	67
Chapter Six: The Emerging Christ	75
Chapter Seven: Unveiling Christos	89

Foreword
by Lee Irwin

Here is a book about the "golden light of Christ" bursting forth creatively into written words and ideas meant to convey that very same Light. David Spangler has a unique and gifted way of making the invisible visible and the visible intimate to what we often cannot see but which is, nevertheless, present. In this book, his written words become a testimony to that presence that "lights up the world" in the form of the inner Christos, the Solar Logos. The cover, by Jeremy Berg, shows us the path into that light as a soul opening encounter in which we can each recognize the sacredness within self and others. The story is one of discovery, an unveiling that reveals the immediacy and vitality of the Christos that lives within each of us, calling us to manifest that potential.

David writes that the "Christ Event is on-going" and "is part of a larger process, which is the incarnation of the World-Soul." The incarnation of the World-Soul has many incarnational teachers and traditions, and among these the Christ is described as an ever-evolving presence which each person can access and which is part of the shared transformation of sacred awareness in a global context. In the same way, Buddhists can find the "inner Buddha," Hindu the "inner Krishna", and Daoists the "inner Lao-Tzu" or "inner Guanyin," Goddess of mercy, or in a western esoteric sense, the "inner Sophia." Thus, each tradition offers its own contribution to such World Soul development. In the Christ-Event, love, compassion, healing, and the care of others are primary expressions of the deep Christos potential, and this forth-coming is an emergence into forms of expression empowered by that sacred presence.

The encounter with the Christ-Event as inner

transformation is, as David teaches, a matter of soul-becoming through a realization of the indwelling presence of the sacred, not simply within oneself, but within others, and within the world and cosmos at large. The Christ-spirit, the indwelling Christos, is a shared reality, permeating increasingly diverse collectives as well as the whole of creation. The unique figure of Yeshu'a as the Christ, "anointed" in spirit, and present within each of us as we attune to that image, is a light source that supports evolutionary transformation through actual incarnations, through individual efforts, and consistent practices. And this is a book of such practices, guided mediations, visualizations, and actions directed toward the solicitation of that inner awakening to the Christ presence. Soul work is not always easy, it takes effort, but the best efforts are guided by inspirations and clarity of thought, and David offers us an abundance of both.

A central metaphor in this work is one of beads on a thread, which is interpreted differently in different contexts – but primarily it is the Christ-thread (as a manifestation of the higher Self-thread) that links various lives, or states, or levels of soul development. If we cut the thread, the beads fall away but the luminous thread remains, the woven strand of the Christos-Self. Here we can see the Mystery – how that thread is not only a circle but a strand in the net of creation, woven threads linked to a multitude of other threads. This net spreads out to encompass the whole of reality, floating in the Sea of Light Ever-Lasting and empowered by the deep Sacred. In such a weaving, the World-Soul is amplified and enhanced by each light strand, each individual realization. It is also a prayer thread, a subtle thread of transmission connecting each soul to its Source, empowering with grace the reborn "I" (eye) that sees and knows that Source through the Christos. As David writes, "Christ is the will within that thread to be unobstructed and graceful in its expression."

Another aspect of the Christ-energy is the "activity of wholeness" that leads to and promotes creativity and the discovery of new meaning and values. We are all in process, undergoing evolutionary transformations and the Christ-Consciousness is both a guide and an opening that can bring the Unmanifest into Manifestation. The subtle interplay between what is forthcoming and what is yet unmanifest requires us to open to that higher Self imaged by the Christos in order to direct our intention towards positive expressions of sacredness. For me that image has long been the Sophianic-Christ, the sacred marriage of the Christos, love and compassion, with Sophia, feminine wisdom and grace. Such love and wisdom, united in the heart as an alchemical union, breathes life into the spark of Self and ignites a subtle flame whose light and warmth illumines the soul with a living sense of "fiery presence." And yet, there are many other forms, images, manifestations, all of which can lead to that very same presence.

David's gift, his words and teachings, are also a Manifestation, another example of how the Christos-Spirit can act to inspire and illumine a shared understanding through teachings that require each individual to adapt, create, and discover for herself or himself, the beauty and power of his words. The center of this work is love, joyful and kind, a love that communicates the sacred in a smile, a gesture, and act of care or concern. Authentic spiritual manifestation refers to the everyday world of interactions, personal relations, family concerns, and meeting the stranger with that very same love. The deep Christos may be esoteric, but the living Christos is the "now moment" as we move through our day, encountering unlimited opportunities to bring forth the Christos in unique manifestations of love and care "at the open edge of transformation."

Another key concept is emergence. This term references creative becoming as a process of unending discovery in which the "I" becomes a means by which the Christo is unveiled. This unveiling, as an act of creative love, has no one form, only unending diverse fractals of the Christ-Self expressed through adaption to real life circumstances. This is our challenge, not to become fixated by collective ideas or beliefs, but to continue the great work of embodying the creative love of the Christ-spirit as we live moment-by-moment, unveiling and "quickening" that hidden potential. As David writes, "all incarnations are manifestations of the sacred" – if so, then every spiritual tradition incarnates, in varying ways, through diverse names and forms, that same hidden potential of sacredness. We are all "sons and daughters of God Indwelling."

Emergence then is a global, multi-traditional and trans-traditional process, and in the global context of "sacred discourses" the *UnVeiled* Christos is a luminous reference to the deeper mystery of collective World-Soul transformation. The Christos radiates a luminous light as the fully expressive "I" that sees and acts in alignment with the sacred in whatever form or response that potential manifests. The "will-to-connect" leads to an unveiling that reveals both the uniqueness and the collaborative nature of connection, what we each bring to the conversation or activity of discovering the sacred together. Emergence is a shared forthcoming, a resonance between individuals sharing a similar light as our "innate universality." We may all bring a different candle, different colors, forms, smells, and shapes, but the light is similar and the wick is sacredness. Through David's exploration of the Christos theme, we can see ever more clearly how our light, his light, and the light yet to come, blend and merge into a shared illumination, opening our eyes ("I") to the ongoing challenges of incarnation and spiritual embodiment. That shared light burns brightly in this luminous book! Thank You, David!

Lee Irwin / Sirr al-Basir
Mediations on Christ. Lorian Press, 2016.
Sophos Ontology: On Post-Traditional Spirituality. Lexington Press 2024

Introduction

This book originates as a transcript of an online class I was asked to present twenty years ago, in 2005. It presents a particular view of the Christ, one that informs my own life and which I felt might be helpful to others.

For me, the Christ is always an emergent—or should I say, emerging—phenomenon, a mythic and spiritual image and presence that is not static but an evolving companion to our own evolving consciousnesses. I do not believe there is a final or complete definition of just what Christ is. It is a sacred landscape that reveals itself to us in ever greater degree the more we are open to exploring it as a living presence within us and within the world. Our perspective and understanding of the meaning of Christ broadens and deepens as we ourselves broaden and deepen in our spiritual and everyday embodied life.

Many years ago, I was sitting in my bedroom when I had a vision of a being of Light who appeared and said to me, "The time will come when the word 'Christ' and the word 'Person' will mean the same thing."

In other words, the Christ is not something outside of us, a force acting from some distant heaven, but the seed of the sacredness of who we really are. It is a symbol of our birthright, a divine ordinariness that participates and unfolds in our everyday life as we become the Light that is the fundamental core of each of us.

Twenty years ago, I felt I wanted to communicate this idea to those who might be interested in exploring its possibilities with me, people who wanted to discover in their own unique, sovereign personhood the presence of the Beloved, the Christ within their own sacredness. With this in mind, I created this class, structuring it around an exercise that made use of four different images of the Christ. The purpose of this exercise was to enable an individual to "unveil" within her- or himself the sacred identity of Christos that is hidden in so many of us behind the traditional images of Christ.

Recently, my good friend and colleague, Jeremy Berg, rediscovered this transcript in the Lorian archives and formatted it in the form of a book. Reading it, I was surprised with what I had offered twenty years earlier, as in the work of developing Incarnational Spirituality, I had totally forgotten about it and about the exercises it offered. It seemes as pertinent now as it did then.

It will become apparent, I trust, that the Christ as I present it here is much more than a religious figure, one exclusive to a single spiritual tradition. I could just as easily refer to it as the "Buddha within," or the "Inner Krishna," or any other spiritual exemplar. The Christos for me is much more than an image of any kind, though imagery and imagination may be the way through which we initially grasp it. It is who we are as incarnate spiritual beings, uniting in ourselves "heaven" and "earth."

As such, it is very much part of the perspective of a universal and immanent spirituality offered by Incarnational Spirituality.

This book is essentially original transcript of that long-ago class. That class was born from a desire to share the blessings I have felt from participation in what I experience as the ongoing Christ Event in the world, a trans-religious Event of acknowledging and embodying our sacred personhood that is as fresh and vital as it was two thousand years ago. It is an Event in which we are all participating. May this book be a blessing to you.

David Spangler

Chapter One:
Sacredness

As a beginning, let me explain what I mean by the words "sacred" and "sacredness."

Sacred for me is a term for the generative mystery from which creation emerges. I use it as a term to mean both the Unmanifest and the Manifest acting together in a co-creative way.

The usual cosmological view is that the Manifest emerges from the Unmanifest, that God creates the cosmos, that the universe emanates forth from a primal source which is beyond all human understanding, since the finite cannot understand nor encompass the infinite.

I share this usual view up to a point. But my understanding and experience is that the Ultimate Source, Ground of Being, Unmanifest, Creator, etc. (whatever term you like), does not create in the same sense that a potter would make a pot or an artist a painting or a writer a novel. It doesn't "make" something. Rather it becomes something. It is an act of incarnation, of taking on a different form or more precisely, expressing as a different form.

So, what we have, in my view, is a Presence that actively is, and its *isness* has two expressions: the Unmanifest and the Manifest. Both are expressions of this single active, creative, generative Presence. Both express a primal quality of being, rather than one being the cause and the other being simply the result of that cause. A partnership emerges that is co-creative, but also, there is a unity of expression in which this creative, generative activity is as much in the Manifest, though in a different way, as it is in the Unmanifest.

A metaphor for me of this relationship is a child. A child comes physically into being as a result of sexual union. My wife, Julia, and I are the physical causes of our children's bodies. But all our children carry in new ways our genetic lineage, and once a child appears, he or she is not simply a creation, an appendage, a product. He or she is a source in his or her own right. He or she is their own "I", their own beingness, their own sovereignty. At some point in their development, our children will become partners to Julie and me. (Actually, our children are co-creative partners even as infants, but as they mature, they become more deliberate and mindful in that partnership.)

Thus, once the Manifest emerges from the Unmanifest (or however that primal differentiation and emergence took place), it is not simply a product, a thing the Unmanifest has made, but an incarnation, a new expression of whatever the Unmanifest is. For "Unmanifest" and "Manifest" are only relative terms that we use to attempt to describe something that may be inherently indescribable: the Sacred.

Another metaphor is that of Light. This is so often used as to be a cliche, but we know that Light can manifest the characteristics of both a particle and a wave, yet, it is neither. What it "really" is, is Light, whatever that is.

In a similar fashion, I see the Sacred as Manifest and Unmanifest, as a Co-Incarnation, and what it "really" is, is the Sacred. I use the terms "Sacred" and "Sacredness" in much the same way a physicist uses the term "Light."

Sacred and sacredness are activities to me, not just states of being or conditions. The sacred, which is the primal condition of beingness and creativity active as both Unmanifest and Manifest, wave and particle, is never static. It is always active, flowing, moving, doing, "incarnating". Analogously, this is why in incarnational spirituality, I teach that an incarnation is not an event or a condition (as in "I was born," or "I have a body, hence I'm incarnated") but a continuous activity, an engagement with life in one form or another.

In that sense, "incarnation" and "sacred" are similar, if not the same activities.

I want to suggest that Manifest and Unmanifest are relative terms, not absolute definitions. The Unmanifest may simply be what we cannot see or know: it is not manifest in a way that is accessible or apprehensible to us. We have theologically, cosmologically, this sense of a one-way flow: the Manifest universe emerging from the Unmanifest, with the former being a "creation," a product, while the latter is a "source" or a "creator." That may indeed be the relationship, but it doesn't preclude our Manifest universe being an Unmanifest source for another universe (indeed, this is a recognized concept in modern astrophysical cosmology, that universes and cosmos may be springing off from this one).

All I really want to do here is shake up our mental viewpoints so we begin to see in less linear and time-bound ways and can get the felt sense that the primal act of generativity and creation—the primal act of sacredness—is happening right now, in us and around us, and not, like the "Big Bang", in some far distant past. Yes, we may have emerged from the Unmanifest, the Generative Mystery that is God, but as soon as we did, we became part of that Mystery, an incarnation of that Mystery, a source of generativity ourselves, not just an effect of it.

Now, part of my focus has been on incarnation, both in a personal human sense—what does it mean for us to be incarnate and how do we do it: what is the structure of an incarnation—and in a more universal sense: the nature of incarnation as a universal activity of sacredness.

Sacredness is not just one thing. It is many manifestations of a primal activity. One such manifestation is that force that elaborates and develops creation: the force of evolution, growth, emergence, unfoldment, creativity, etc. This is analogous to the forces of life and biology within our bodies that enable them to develop from single celled zygotes into babies, toddlers, children, teenagers, and adults, and from one person to couples to families to tribes to cities to nations to planets, and so forth.

Another manifestation, though, is that which deepens the presence of sacredness within creation, that deepens the incarnation, quickening it, heightening it, giving it interiority, giving it coherency and integrity, giving it sovereignty and presence, awakening its partnering capacity with the Unmanifest, awakening its capacity to know itself, to be sacred in consciousness and awareness as well as in simple growth and elaboration.

When my child is born, we are immediately in a co-creative relationship. He or she changes me from the get-go, and I become a new person. But as my child matures and develops, there comes a time when he or she can partner with me in a very deliberate way, when we can have an adult relationship and friendship. This is a different kind of co-creativity; one based on mindfulness and depth of experience. My child becomes another form of "Spangler-ness" reflecting back on my form of "Spangler-ness," and together we manifest a new dimension of "Spangler-ness."

What makes this possible is love. By love, I mean not only affection and caring and all the feelings that we usually associate with this word, but also, a sense of shared identity acting to nourish and fulfill its different manifestations AND to manifest its unity.

This activity of sacredness that loves, holds, maintains, deepens, and furthers the depth, the interiority, the sense of unity, the partnering, the co-creativity, the shared identity between the two aspects of the sacred which I call the

Unmanifest and the Manifest, is what I'm calling Christ. It is the primal, universal activity of Christ.

HOLDING THE SACRED

To hold something is to make it accessible, like a bowl holds water that I can then drink. It provides it a space for its activity and presence. Holding the sacred, in my terminology, means to make it accessible and to provide a space for its activity and presence in my life and consciousness.

I define Christ as that which can hold the presence of the "I", the sacred identity, thus making it available to us. Now I should say something more about this "I".

As I understand it, "I" is an experience of the sacred that emphasizes the character of self-ness. I think of it as the individualization of the sacred. When we as individuals emerge as "units" or co-creative monads of sacred activity, there is in this emergence a sense of self or "I" which becomes our unique expression and incarnation of sacredness. From this "I" emerges our spirit, which may have a long history of evolution before it ever becomes associated with humanity, and from this spirit in turn comes what I call our "Humanity Soul." This is our spirit giving expression to and participating in a particular sacred idea and activity whose manifestation is a cosmic, universal field of energy and consciousness I call "Humanity." When this "Cosmic Humanity" becomes engaged with Gaia and the life and energy of this world, our "Humanity Soul" gives rise to a human soul, which in turn becomes the source for our personal incarnations in the physical world.

We are part of a spectrum, a continuum, of individuated consciousness that extends far beyond this world, but which is anchored in the experience and presence of "I". More precisely, if I use the metaphor of a necklace of beads, our various incarnations (and not just our physical human ones but our incarnations in realms of soul, spirit and cosmos as well) are the beads, but the "I" is the thread which holds them together. And this thread is accessible to each bead, to each incarnation.

Here's a diagram:

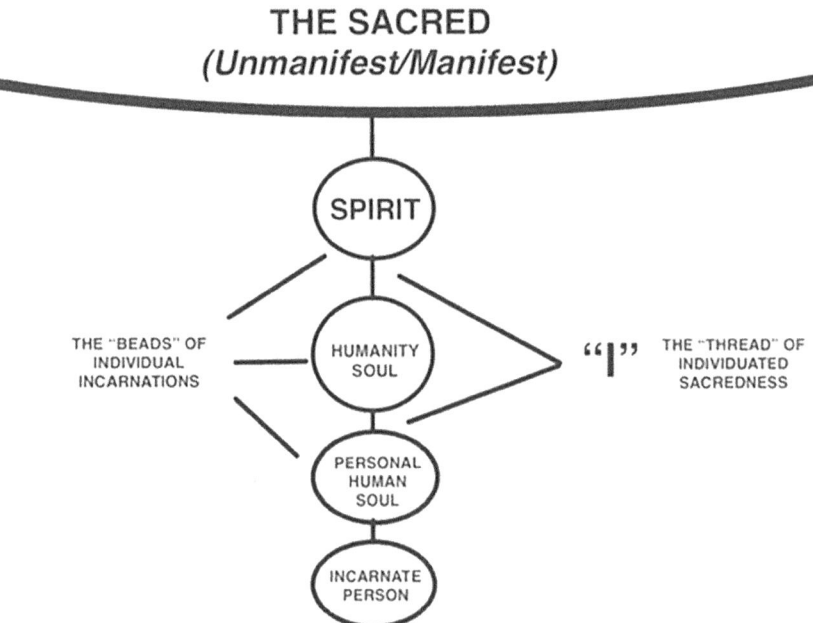

Simply put, "I" is our individualized activity of sacredness. It manifests as much through our human incarnate personalities, such as David in my case, as it does through any "higher" or precursor state, such as my, David's, soul.

Having this sacredness intrinsically active within us, though, is not the same as being aware of it and consciously participating in and embodying it. For this to happen, this sacredness needs to be accessible to us, and this is what the activity of Christos does.

In all the worlds of creation, my understanding is that Christ makes sacredness—the consciousness of the depth dimension, the coherency of the cosmos, the activity of love, wholeness, and partnering—accessible to the realms of form and growth. It makes the Unmanifest accessible to the Manifest and vice versa. It is the Light that holds particle and wave together as a single phenomenon which in turn allows them to express as separate phenomena.

In my own life, I encountered Christ in two distinct ways. The first, when I was a child, was through the church, the bible, Sunday school. In this context, Christ is contained within (and limited to) the personage of Jesus. I even projected the image of Jesus onto inner beings I would encounter. As a child, I would be visited occasionally by shining beings, and I always thought of them as being Jesus, since that was the only image I had from my outer world to represent someone who radiated Light.

This was definitely Christ as other. Yet, there was always something about Jesus that deeply affected me and stirred my soul. There was an inner reality that I could feel but didn't know how to articulate, that went beyond the figure of Jesus. To try to understand and engage with this unknown reality, I would imaginatively project myself back into the time of Jesus, as if I could encounter him and discover what was there. I had a child's map of Jesus's world and all the places he went and worked tacked above my bed. This wasn't one of those Rand McNally type maps that you can get at gas stations; it was an imaginative depiction of the houses, villages, lakes, roads, and cities that he visited. I would gaze up at that map and imagine myself walking those ancient roads with him and being part of his life, trying to draw near to the Mystery that I felt intuitively was there but couldn't quite grasp with my mind.

But while I yearned for what Christ represented—I knew intuitively it meant something important to me, more important than just church or bible studies or religion itself—it still remained the other, like imagining myself (which I also did as a kid) visiting Metropolis and meeting Clark Kent, Lois Lane, and, of course, Superman himself!

My first encounter with Christ as a force in the universe, as a real presence and not simply as a marvelous person in bible stories, occurred when I was thirteen. It happened quite unexpectedly as I was out hiking in the desert around Phoenix, Arizona. It was not an encounter with a being—with an Other—but with a golden Light that simultaneously surrounded me and burst out from within me. And it came with a very clear message: "If you would know Christ, you must know the Christ you already are."

With these words came a realization that the Christ being referred to was not the Presence that incarnated as Jesus, nor was it any form of avataric expression; I was not being told that I was a Messiah or the Second Coming. Instead, this experience was pointing to something very natural and ordinary already present in me, and in all living beings, something as natural as life itself.

I could not then have articulated it in the way I am doing in this book. I did not have an intellectual concept of Christ as an activity or function. But it was a clear sense of Christ as an innate part of life and consciousness, woven as deeply into the fabric of the universe as the laws of physics and chemistry and as much a part of us as carbon and oxygen. That experience started me along a particular way of understanding Christ.

Now the laws of physics, and the atoms of carbon and oxygen, can be blended to form a blade of grass or a human being. A blade of grass can do things that I cannot (photosynthesis, for one thing, which is a miracle in itself), but I can do things a blade of grass cannot, such as write these words and think about the Christ. We are "other" to each other. But we are also carbon-based life forms engaging in a recognizably similar activity of livingness. I can recognize grass as life, and in that recognition, see that same life as it operates in me. We are not only kin, but we are kin that can empower each other because we resonate to a common livingness.

The activity that is Christ can take many forms as well. To a being who embodies this activity at a planetary or cosmic level, I may be like a blade of grass, but we are still kin. Unless I recognize that kinship, I cannot fully see or know that being. He or she may remain Other to me in a way that does not quicken something inside me because I do not perceive a link between us, other than an abstraction of Oneness in which our differences become lost and void. We are kin in a mutual activity of "Christness."

In this sense, it takes a Christ to recognize a Christ.

It was the "Christness" in the apostles that allowed them to recognize the Christ in Jesus.

This is not abstract philosophical or theological theory to me but an application. Whatever capacity I have had in my life to connect with the Christ and explore its mysteries has come directly out of my ability and willingness to discern Christ in me, not as a presence per se but as an activity. It comes out of seeing incarnation in a particular way, not as an Incarnation in the way Jesus is seen as an Incarnation—a special descent of the Solar Logos into the earth within a singular human being—but as a sacred activity in itself. Every incarnation is the sacred taking form through the activity of Christ.

I see Christ in a variety of ways. There is Christ as activity, which we are focusing upon in this book. This is, to me, a "veiled Christos," the Christos we often do not see simply because it is so natural, organic, and innate in us; it is so much a part of who we are that we overlook it. My hope is that this book will unveil this inner Christos.

Then there is Christ as presence, which emerges as the Christ, as a natural, universal activity becomes self-conscious and aware. Christ as Presence is the Christ as Activity now filled with mind and heart and awakened to Identity. It is Christ as Presence that we most often think of when we think of Christos.

Thirdly, there is Christ as Deed. A Deed is a conscious act (not simply an activity) of Christ that affects and transforms something in the world in some manner. A Deed of Christ might be to awaken the unconsciousness of Christ as Activity into the consciousness of Christ as Presence. Or it might be a specific deed of healing or illumination. I think of the incarnation of Jesus as a Deed of Christ which had a profound evolutionary affect upon humanity and the world. A Deed of Christ is what a Christ as Presence does.

This oversimplifies, I know, and these three overlap. There is always more to life and spirit than the categories we assign to them, but as a broad perspective, I find these three distinctions useful.

My point is this: I have found that when people awaken to Christ as an activity within themselves, as part of their incarnations, rather than as another outside themselves, there can be, as I said earlier, a shift. This shift is not so much one of invoking and taking on Christ as it is of inhabiting one's own incarnation and self in a new way. The incarnation becomes Christic because we experience how it holds our "I". We can experience how little ordinary things we do can be seen—and actually are—expressions of a Christic activity. They may not be as dramatic as the miracles of Jesus, but they are the stuff of which life and the world are made.

The purpose for me of exploring and "unveiling" Christ as a natural activity, a function within creation that can manifest as a variety of related activities (all of which have their roots in love), is that it gives us a starting point of kinship from which to explore and engage with Christ as Presence, consciousness, and sacredness. There is no limit that I'm aware of as to where that exploration and development may go. Jesus said we could and would do as he did and greater things as well.

I realize that what I am asking you, my Reader, to do in this book is to encounter your own incarnation in a new way, using the image of Christ as a way to do so. As I said earlier, I could use different images to accomplish the same thing: the "inner Buddha," for example, or the "Inner Moses." I am not talking about a religious figure exclusive to one spiritual tradition but a spirit that is universally within all of them. But I have experienced this as an expression of Christos, so that is the image that comes most naturally to me.

For me, love is at the heart of what Christ is, or I could say, Christ is at the heart of love, so yes, the more I can love, the more I express a resonance with Christ. The more I love, the more I unveil the Christ or the sacredness within.

Chapter Two:
Thinking About Christ

The first thing I would like us to do is to think about thinking about Christ. Here's why.

The idea and image of Christ does not come to us unadorned or without history. It is one of those ideas and images that has occupied the thinking and feeling lives of millions of humans for over two thousand years. So much has already been written, so much has already been said, so much has already been thought and felt about the Christ before us, and we inherit that in one way or another. Christ is indirectly, if not directly, part of the environment in which we live.

It's not as if we come to this subject with a wholly clean slate. It's not as if I were talking to you about the sex life of the South Pacific trivalve clam or the medicinal properties of the boola-boola plant that only grows from October to December on the western slopes of the Andes in Peru. Christ is part of the thought and feeling life of Western culture, and even if we are not Christian or hardly ever (or never) go to church, it's not an influence or an idea we can totally escape.

In this book, I want us to explore some new ideas about the Christ. I want us to think in new ways about old ideas concerning the Christ. What do we need to do in our own mental and feeling lives in order to do that?

As you think about your various images and thoughts about Jesus and Christ, I'm sure it becomes apparent at how broad this subject matter is and how deeply it may have penetrated your thinking, feeling, and spiritual life in one way or another. That is just a fact, but it is one I wish you to be aware of as we go on.

What I wish is for us to engage with the idea and the

energies of the Christ as freshly as possible so that that idea and those energies have a chance to engage with us in new and dynamic ways. Our greatest challenge will be the tyranny of the familiar, the temptation to say to ourselves, "Oh, I already know about that." This is made ever more tempting because we will be using old familiar words.

Therefore, we need to be mindful of what we already know or feel, the images we already hold, and while respecting them, to step past them into a clear space. It's like seeing the twin of someone we know well. The visage is familiar, but it's not quite the same person.

PARTICIPATING IN CHRIST

I want to emphasize that this book is definitely about discovering ways in which we participate in the Christ event and in "Christ-ness," whatever that turns out to be. This is not a book in Christology in the usual sense. It's an exploration into a mystery within our own incarnations, a discovery of something innate in us and in our world, using Christ-flavored images to do so. Our objective is to understand, recognize, and embody a characteristic of our lives, a quality, activity, or motion intrinsic to us.

In exploring this, I am going to divide each chapter text into three parts: Mythic Story, Formative Activity, and Personal Embodiment.

Mythic Story

This is where I will present text material in the form of a story. I suppose this could also be seen as a presentation of some of the esoteric or inner perspectives on the Christ Deed and drama. However, I think of it more as an impressionistic rendering of images and energies I've tuned into over the years in considering this topic. For me, the Christ event is so complex and multi-layered that I'm not sure a simple "esoteric history" or "esoteric Christianity" can be presented. Nevertheless, in this section of text, I'll give it a go!

This is the storyteller, the mystic, and the esotericist in me having a fling!

Formative Activity

In this section of the text, I'll explore the Christ as a sacred, formative (creative and incarnational) activity. The tone here will be less storytelling and more like a scientific exploration and hypothesis. Here is where we consider the various elements of the Christ as energies, activities, capacities, and the like which, like fractals, are replicated throughout the various layers and manifestations of the Cosmos.

This is the biologist, the chemist, the physicist, and the magician in me having a go!

Personal Embodiment

This is the text in which we look at how we can embody the story and activities of Christos in our everyday lives. This is the most important part, the part that has to live for you and me if this book is to succeed. After all, I would like us all to leave this book with a sense of participating in (and even of being) Christos, not just with a new set of ideas, words, and images as part of some Christology we have learned and can think about.

Finally, the term "Veiled Christos" suggests an image of Christ that is hidden but which may be unveiled. In this instance, the historical Christ and the images we hold of him and of his incarnation form the veil behind which, in each of us in our incarnations, is the Christos that is hidden.

Let us see what veils we can remove and what Christos we can reveal.

THE CHRIST EVENT

In this section we have two key ideas to consider.

First, the Christ Event is still ongoing, and we are participating in it.

Second, the Christ Event is part of a larger event or process which is the incarnation of the World Soul and—within that and related to that—the incarnation of Humanity (and, of course, of we individual human beings). This larger Event is facilitated by all aspects of humanity, spirituality and science, commerce and art; it is advanced by all the spiritual teachers, saints, and exemplars of our species. It is as much an Islamic and a Jewish, a Buddhist and a Hindu, a Pagan and an indigenous Shamanic enterprise as it is a Christian one,

Though I do not mean this as an exact biological analogy, in a fashion the Christ Event is like puberty. Puberty is the beginning of our reproductive adulthood, and that capacity to reproduce remains with us for most of the rest of our lives. Puberty is the awakening of a capacity, and the Christ Event may be seen in this way as well. Such a capacity is not a one-time event but is ongoing.

Let me emphasize this: the Christ Event is ongoing. It is happening now, and we are all part of it to the extent that we choose to be so—and choose to embody love—whatever our religious or spiritual persuasion. (Again, I could, if that were my background and experience, call this the "Buddha Event" or the "Islamic Event" or the "Prophets Event," whatever term best expresses for me the fullness and promise of the spiritual tradition to which I feel aligned.)

The Christ Event is often traditionally seen as an event of redemption. We will consider this in more detail later. But for now, I affirm that it is much more than that and operates in a much larger context than simply dealing with the "sinfulness" or "fall" of humanity.

The ongoingness and currency of the Christ Event transcends time. It is more than ripples extending outward through time from an impact point in Israel two thousand and more years ago.

I realize I have not—and am not—defining what I mean by "The Christ Event." I want to leave that open for right now. Let's just assume it means "whatever was done by the Christ, including the appearance and incarnation of Jesus." Later, I'll define it more explicitly, but that will actually be towards the end of our book.

For now, though, consider the Christ Event as a sphere. Perhaps we can think of it as an orange.

When an orange sits on my counter, it does so as something complete and whole, a round fruit. If, however, I take a knife to it, I can cut it into circular slices which can then be laid out in a line across the counter. The pieces at either end will be very small circles while the middle piece will be the biggest circle. That is because the diameter or thickness of the orange increases as we move towards its middle and then decreases again as we move to the edges.

If I do not slice the orange, I see it as a single round fruit. If I do slice the orange, I see it as a line of circles of varying sizes. Each slice appears separate from each other, and the two end slices are the farthest away from each other.

In this metaphor, the knife is our perception and experience of time. It is our vision honed and sharpened to an edge, an edge that can slice what in fact is a single energy system into a series of related events progressing through time.

FLATLAND

A very good illustration is in the book *Flatland: A Romance of Many Dimensions*, a fable written by Edwin

Abbott, published in 1884. It tells the story of a land of two dimensions inhabited by squares, triangles, circles, and the like. Nothing has more than two dimensions, hence it is a flat land.

The hero of this fable is a square. He lives an ordinary flatlander life until one evening he dreams of a sphere. In effect, he has risen in consciousness to another realm, one that has three dimensions. In such a realm, squares become cubes, triangles become pyramids, and circles become spheres.

At first, he has no idea what he is seeing or what has happened to him. But gradually he grasps the idea of this strange new third dimension—height—and with it, a whole new perspective on himself is born.

He realizes that if his new friend, the sphere, were to physically visit his world, none of his fellow flatlanders would be able to see its third dimension. Instead, they would experience it as a series or progression of circles, just like the orange slices. The only way they could perceive its fullness would be through time. So, the sphere would appear as a sequence of events that would appear separate yet related. However, if they were to gain the capacity to see into three dimensions, those events would coalesce into a single event or being.

I won't go into the rest of the story, save to say that it is charming and well worth a visit.

Relative to the inner worlds, we are like the flatlanders. We see and experience things within a framework of four dimensions, three of space and one of time. The inner worlds possess progressively more dimensions to their structures (as, of course, do the beings that live upon them). A spiritual event cannot be fully perceived only through three- or four-dimensional eyes. It will appear as something else, something comprehensible to us. Metaphorically, it would be like seeing a series of events rather than as a single event, like a line of orange slices rather than as an orange.

To me, this is the nature of the Christ Event. It is an action or a presence that is still occurring, though we tend to see it as having occurred two thousand years ago, with effects that we are still feeling today like waves hitting a beach. This means that we are as much in the presence of the Christ and in the midst of the Christ Event now as were those people who lived in Israel two thousand plus years ago.

That is the context in which I offer this book. How we relate to Christ—and to the Christos within us—depends on whether we can see the whole orange or only a slice or two.

EXERCISE ONE:

The first exercise I would like you to do is very simple and requires hardly any effort. I would like you to take a moment and think about Christ. Specifically, I would like you to list some images, thoughts, and ideas that arise in you when you hear or think the word "Christ" or "Jesus Christ".

Four or five words or phrases is fine, ten should be the max.

Once you have your list, I'd like you to go over it and for each image or idea that you have put down, reflect on the impact it has on you. What does it feel like? What does it make you feel like? Where are you, so to speak, in relationship to that idea or image? What is its felt sense within you? What does it evoke from you? How important is it to you? Do you see that image as a slice of the orange or as the whole orange?

EXERCISE TWO:

Referring back to the text that we are as much in the midst of the Christ Event—and as much in the presence of the Christ—as a person living in Galilee two thousand plus years ago, how does this idea make you feel? Does it change anything within you? Does it change any way you look out at the world? Do you feel an energy or an inner presence that you might not have before? What is the effect of this idea within you?

EXERCISE THREE:
Imagine yourself standing on the street.

The Christos appears coming down the street. How do you feel?

Christ approaches you. Does anything in you resist or feel awkward? What might that be? Why?

Stopping next to you, Christ touches and awakens something within you. What might that be? What part of you? What quality has been awakened? What aspect of yourself?

To begin building an inner field of resonance with our subject matter, spend time this week with the thought of Christ. Go through your day as if Christ is with you, within you. Observe how you feel, what happens, etc.

Chapter Three:
Redemption And The Christ Of History

In the course of this book, we are going to consider the Christ from different angles, attuning to each as we go along. Then we'll put all these angles together into a single exercise or ritual focusing on how the Christ lives in each of us uniquely and individually.

At this time, let us consider the Christ of History, the Christ that we all know from two thousand years of Christian tradition, teaching, yearning, imaging, praying, and believing. Even this Christ of History can take many forms, as the divisions within Christianity bear witness. There are competing Christologies, ranging from the most esoteric to the most mundane.

I choose to focus on one particular aspect of Christ, the one that is probably most common and well-known: Christ as Redeemer and Savior and the Christ Event as one of redemption. It will serve as our first entry point into the mystery of Christos and its unveiling.

THE MYTHIC STORY

All creatures—all beings, animate or inanimate, organic or inorganic—possess sacredness. Humanity possesses the capacity to be conscious and self-reflective of this sacredness. We can be aware not only of our environment and its incarnate nature but also only aware of the supersensible, energetic, or spiritual aspects of that environment (or of itself). We can also awaken to and be aware of our participation in the sacred act of incarnation and creation from which the cosmos is always emerging.

We can be aware of our sacredness as the quality and

capacity called "I". This is the Self from which our ordinary felt sense of self arises.

Coming to awareness of this "I" within us is one of the evolutionary tasks of humanity. Another is to recognize this "I"—this co-creative participation in sacredness—within the body and life of the earth and to contribute to its awakening within other beings as much as is possible and appropriate. A third great evolutionary task is to embody this "I" in co-creative, co-emergent, co-evolutionary partnership with the "I" within the World Soul, the Logos of the Earth.

Humanity is a complex being. We are what I call a "crossroads" being in that various different streams of evolution converge and are synthesized within us. Part of our evolutionary goal is to develop the capacity of synthesis as an expression of love. As elements of the formative, mineral, vegetable, and animal kingdoms combine in us, something new emerges: a unique pattern that can contain the "I" within earthly incarnation in a way that makes it accessible to all these other streams and kingdoms of consciousness. Part of humanity must, of necessity, evolve from within the earth itself in order to be in communion and empathetic resonance with the rest of earthly life.

Gaia—the Earth Logos or World Soul—is also part of a stellar and cosmic environment. It contains within itself capacities to connect with and hold energies arising from these expanded domains. Consequently, humanity as part of Gaia must also have within itself these same capacities. Some of these are also evolved from within the earth experience, but others are brought into the mix from humanity's own cosmic nature and from cosmic and stellar beings who have injected parts of themselves—parts of their own consciousnesses and energies—into the evolution of humanity. (For a fuller treatment of this, please see my book, *Partnering with Spirit*.)

The effect of all this gathering and mixing of different elements and energies into humanity is to give birth to an emergent consciousness that is planetary yet more than planetary, a consciousness capable of manifesting the sacred "I" both individually and collectively. It gives us the tools and capacities we need to achieve the three tasks of planetary evolution I described above.

However, this evolution and emergence is not without challenge. It is much easier to develop as a "pure" being (like, say, an elemental of water that only has to deal with being water) than as an amalgamation and synthesis of many different forces and elements. Humanity is not "impure," but until it achieves a holistic synthesis, it can be pulled in different energetic directions and can become incoherent as it strives to blend what can be competing attractions.

Incoherency is our great evolutionary challenge: the failure to synthesize, blend, create wholeness, and become coherent within ourselves and in relationship with our world. Incoherency generates "noise", static, and friction that make coherency more difficult. We can get sidetracked and stuck in parts of ourselves, failing to achieve wholeness.

When incoherency happens in us, we can transmit it through our attitudes and actions into the world. The world soul also, works to achieve coherency on a planetary scale. Its task is similar to that of humanity in this regard. Incoherency can arise within the field of the world as well as within humanity. Not all incoherency is humanity's fault, and sometimes incoherency within the world makes it harder for humanity to find coherency within itself. Sometimes it is the reverse.

The challenge is that the parts of us can dominate and speak louder than the Whole of us, our "I." Initially, at least, the "I" is a "still, small voice" of synthesis and coherency within us.

To summarize, we have the following dynamics going on over the course of human and planetary evolution:

We have the gradual development of an emergent consciousness within humanity capable of recognizing, attuning to, and holding the "I" within its incarnate planetary self.

This emergent consciousness is not "pure" but complex and mixed in order to heighten humanity's capacity to relate to all forces within planetary evolution and mediate the "I" to them. Humanity has an evolutionary capacity for synthesis and coherency.

This capacity for synthesis and coherency, however, does not appear in a perfected and fully capable state. It is something we learn and develop, and in the process, we also, experience and generate states of incoherency.

These states and energies of incoherency can be swiftly healed and corrected where there is adequate flow of spiritual energy and synthesis, but otherwise, they can accumulate and become obstructions to that flow. Strong parts arise in us that mimic the "I" and attempt to create coherency, but they are not the "I" and thus do not embody coherency as a natural state of being. They always leave something (often their opposite) out of the mix. They lack love. Coherency cannot really be imposed by a single part of us, at least not for very long.

So, competing states of limited coherency, obstructions, unintegrated and incoherent energies, and other challenges arise as part of the natural flux and dynamics of the evolutionary process, both within the world as a whole and within humanity. Life is by its nature exploratory, trying different things out. Not everything is successful.

The challenge arises because on the physical level, at least, qualities of persistence and fixity lead to inertia and habit. Mistakes linger and become obstructions that can generate other mistakes. Humanity can be like a hoarder, hanging on to traumas, memories, attitudes, and behaviors that have long ago ceased to be useful or beneficial (if they ever were). This creates a condition that threatens to become a "permanent" incoherency, like the piled-up boxes and objects in a hoarder's house that make it difficult to move about or find a clear space. This is planetary karma: habit patterns that work against wholeness and an inertial resistance to change.

After a certain point, a person who has become an extreme hoarder may not be able to free themselves from their accumulation. An outside agency may need to come forward to start the process and to enable the hoarder to discover in themselves their own innate power of liberation so that they do not continue the hoarding behavior. They need to discover the "I" that is neither defined by nor dependent upon their possessions and habits and is greater and more creative than either.

Humanity's ability to connect to and embody the sacred "I" in ways that enhance the sacredness within the world is vital, a skill that needs to be awakened and expressed if we are to successfully accomplish our evolutionary contributions to Gaia and its evolution.

At the same time, there are also these challenging conditions and forces arising from what is essentially poor energy hygiene that has allowed an accumulation of karma, habit, and inertia, all "clogging" up the clear flow of living sacred energies. This inner "hoarding" and accumulation makes recognition of and connection to the "I" increasingly difficult. If allowed to continue, humanity's evolution will be greatly slowed down and fragmented as more and more people experience greater and greater difficulty connecting to their innate sacredness; there is even a possibility that humanity's planetary tasks could be aborted.

Something more is needed than just a collective heightening and a gradual unfolding of the innate capacity to hold the "I". Something must enter directly into the incarnational system and into humanity that can directly bring the presence of the "I" into planetary incoherency and begin to shatter and reform its congealing patterns. The "outside agency" must act to help the hoarder clear out his house.

The Christos is the capacity to hold the "I", but it is also a powerful energy field of love, synthesis and coherency. It is a powerful field of Light. And it is this field, esoterically linked to the Solar Logos, that entered the energy field of the earth to begin both the clearing away process and the further awakening and enabling of the liberating "I" or Christos within incarnate humanity.

This field cannot be embodied by a single person. It is a collective event. It begins to intersect with the world centuries before the birth of Jesus, and it continues to intersect with the world today. It is a whole "orange," but with our time-based awareness, we see it as a series of "slices," with a large slice when Jesus lived but with a slice representing our current moment of history as well.

However, given that this is world of particles and individuals, this Christ Event, this Christ Field, also needed to take on a particular expression in a specific individual life in order to be recognized. Since so few people can see the orange, it's important that there be slices that can be seen, and Jesus was one such (though in my understanding, not the only such) slice.

The Christ Field needed to incarnate as the life of a single human individual because it is in the arena of our individual lives that the "I" can unfold; this is where the challenge of replacing incoherency with coherency, fragmentation with wholeness, and negativity with love must be met. So, Christos must be manifested as an individual person as well as a collective field. And that person, exercising the power and presence of the "I," can demonstrate in the context of an individual life the three goals of human evolution in a form accessible to us: the goal of embodying sacredness or the "I" (incarnation), the goal of connecting this presence to the world (stewardship and service), and the goal of partnering and co-creating with the world to shape new futures (making all things new).

This act of incarnation is accomplished by a particular being of high evolution (some esoteric traditions say it is a being from the solar realms) who embodies the collective aspect in partnership with the soul that we know as Jesus to embody the individual emergence and expression.

This act of collective and individual incarnation both starts the clearing away of ancient debris and habits accumulated in the evolutionary process—something we as "hoarders" had lost the power to do own our own.

This is the Redemption.

This redemptive act, carried out by a High Being embodying its own "I" as well as a "solar 'I'", is one of charging humanity and the earth with a quickening of energies that are cleansing and able to confront, disperse, or heal the incoherent energies.

It is this act (and often this Being) that we recognize and refer to as being the Christ Event, an event usually defined in terms of redemption.

But there is a whole other Christ Act or Event that is not redemptive in nature *per se*.

The Redemptive Act makes it more likely that this greater

Act will be received and embodied; it clears a space and quickens the energies for it. This is the Act of awakening individuals to the presence of Christos within them as a power of ongoing and continuous loving energy hygiene. It is a Christ Act that heightens the ability of human beings to connect with their own sacredness so they are less likely to be as vulnerable to the inertia of habit and incoherency. We are heightened in our capacity to achieve coherency, primarily through love.

In my metaphor, this is the act of awakening or restoring within the individual a sense of wholeness such that this person won't feel a need to hoard and will stop doing so. Enabling the emergence of the whole person is a greater act than simply clearing all the junk out of a house, especially if the owner is likely to start hoarding and filling it up with junk again!

The act of redemption seems more dramatic, certainly. The idea of being "saved" can overshadow and obscure the idea of enabling sacredness. Watching a clean-up crew take piles of old stuff out of a hoarder's house can be eye-catching and exciting compared to the quieter and often invisible inner work of healing and restoring wholeness within a person. But in the long run, it's the latter that will make a difference, although the former is necessary to start the process.

FORMATIVE ACTIVITY

In this section, we consider the Christ as a function of the sacred, akin to a natural law or activity like gravity or electromagnetism, part of the structure of creation. It's redemptive quality and action is built into this function.

Incarnation
Incarnation is the act by which the Unmanifest becomes

Manifest, the act through which Cosmos emerges from the Sacred. I prefer this term to "manifestation" or even "creation" because it carries with it the sense of participation and involvement. To me, it conveys that the Manifest universe is not just a product of an act but an expression of a presence in a new form. To incarnate is to "put on flesh," and that is what the Unmanifest does: the Manifest cosmos is the flesh of God.

In this process, there is a force that links the Unmanifest and the Manifest, a continuum, coherency, or consistency of Identity between these two realities. It is this force, in fact, that transforms what could simply be a manifestation into an incarnation: a force of sacred life, the Logos that unites Manifest and Unmanifest into a wholeness. This force or presence is what renders the universe sacred. It anoints the universe with sacredness, with the "I" of God, the Presence of the Generative Mystery. It enables creation in all its forms to hold the "I" of God, to hold and express sacredness.

In my understanding, this force is the Christos.

Difference

In our seeking for oneness, wholeness, and unity, we can overlook the power and importance of difference and separation as part of the incarnational process.

If the Manifest is simply a straightforward copy of the Unmanifest, then, in a way, nothing has happened. There has been no creation. There is no new information. In cybernetic theory, information is described as "the difference that makes a difference". If there is no difference between Unmanifest and Manifest, then is there really anything Manifest?

The words "Unmanifest" and "Manifest" suggest a fundamental difference between two states of being. Something has happened that allows cosmos to emerge, and cosmos—the universe—is not absolutely identical to the Nothing-ness, Void, or Mystery from which it has emerged. If it is, then what has been achieved?

If there is difference, then there is a space for something new to emerge. The relationship between Unmanifest and Manifest generates new information; creation flows. Cosmos becomes a fractal of the Sacred, a self-similar replication that is not an identical copy.

Incarnation as a process is more than replication; it is emergence. It creates difference.

Difference is an essential part of creation, and difference can certainly generate uniqueness and separation. Not separation in the sense of disunity and isolation, but separation in the sense of not being the same thing. The boundaries that separate and create difference can be very thin, beyond our human capacity to discern, and yet still be there. On the other hand, at our level of vibration, life, cosmos, and perception, differences and separation loom large. They are very evident.

It doesn't take much reflection to perceive that a human being is not the same as a tree. Both provide different sets of capacities and information, and together they can generate new information. A house or a boat made of wood is something that doesn't arise naturally; it is an emergent form that appears through the relationship and interaction of a human being and a tree. It represents new learning and new information.

Difference and the relationship between differences that can generate emergence is an important creative process within the Manifest cosmos.

Yet all the difference and diversity within Cosmos is still held in a context of sacredness; it is still filled and anointed with sacredness. It is still an incarnation of the Unmanifest.

It is still an expression of "I". This holding and unity is what the agency and force of Christ as a natural, structural part of creation provides.

Christ is the connective tissue between the Identity of Sacredness and the different manifestations of Sacredness. It aligns the "I" as Being with the expression as activity and form.

Order and Chaos

In the sciences of complexity, life is defined as existing "at the edge of chaos." What is meant by this is that life is an emergent phenomenon that is neither so highly structured that it becomes fixed and static, nor so highly fluid and chaotic that no connections are possible and everything simply disperses into randomness. Some order and fixity are necessary and some chaos and fluidity are necessary in order to allow life to be flexible and growing.

We see order and chaos as opposites and sometimes misidentify them with "good" and "evil," for who likes chaos in their lives (at least beyond a certain point)? But they are not really opposites as much as they are two aspects of a dynamic process, much as light is both a particle and a wave but actually is neither or something for which we have no appropriate word.

Creation manifests through flow and circulation; it depends on friction and resistance, boundaries and limits. Chaos is like the joker that prevents any given structure from becoming too fixed; it opens things up. But order is also a joker that prevents any given flow from being too unformed; it gives focus.

In the course of things, it is possible for local conditions of too much order or too much chaos to develop. Creation is like walking: it is a process of continually falling out of balance. Too much order, and all I do is stand still. Too much chaos and all I do is fall over. But the interaction and balance between the two produces grace and the ability to walk.

However, it is also possible to stagger.

Sometimes, creation staggers and grace is lost.

Misalignment and disconnection

When this happens, there is misalignment and disconnection. Then, in a healthy system, there is a natural balancing action that comes into play, just as there is for us if we stagger when we walk. Ultimately, all beings are aligned to the "I". This force of Christ offers and restores grace. It is a matter of coming back into harmony and alignment with the identity of the sacred pervading all creation. This, too, could be seen as a natural redemptive aspect of Christos.

This restoration of grace can involve a number of specific actions and processes depending on the situation. What has caused the stumble or stagger, so to speak? What is creating the misalignment and disconnection? Is it too much order or too much chaos? Is it the lack of balance? Is there too much inertia moving in one direction? Is the flow of energy blocked? Has it become stagnant? Is something interfering with the alignment with the "I?.

Each level of incarnation has its own way of experiencing the "I" which in turn opens to further and broader ways of experiencing it all the way back to the primal "I" itself. Is this "chain of command" or alignment—what might be called the "Spine of Creation"—now misaligned, blocked, cut off in some way? Is there a "slipped disk" that obstructs the graceful flow of presence from the Unmanifest Mystery through all the levels of cosmic incarnation? What needs to be done to restore grace and flow so that knowledge of, attunement to, and participation with the "I" of the sacred can be restored and enhanced, or so that new experiences of the "I" can emerge?

Redemption

Redemption is defined in my dictionary as "recovering ownership" and "setting free". To redeem is to reclaim and, in effect, to restore. If my back is out, my chiropractor redeems it by putting it straight again so that all my nerves are again in alignment.

Consider the words that go along with redemption: unblocking, forgiving, recovering, reclaiming, re-membering, realigning, unobstructing, and restoring. All of these imply putting things back into flow, back into grace, back into order (or more precisely, back into the balanced relationship of order and chaos!). In our context here, they suggest realignment with the sacred, the "I", that is within us.

Redemption and Beyond

We see the Christ as the Spirit of Incarnation that holds and maintains the graceful and balanced flow and presence of "I" or sacredness through all the levels and forms of incarnate manifestation, so that each level and form becomes a fractal of the generative Source and mystery. Each level and form of incarnation throughout the cosmos becomes a point of expression of sacredness, creativity, and emergence.

If I think of all my levels of incarnation—from the cells in my body through my psyche to the sacredness at the edge of the Unmanifest—as beads on a necklace of incarnation, then Christ is the thread that connects them and makes them a wholeness. But it is also the force within that thread that seeks to unkink and unknot it when it gets tangled and flow is impaired. Christ is the will within that thread to be unobstructed and graceful in its expression.

When kinks and knots appeared in the human thread and the planetary threads, the nature of Christ is to reclaim the flow, reclaim the grace, reclaim the straightness of the thread. This manifests as some form of redemptive action or actions.

Redemption is a natural function that seeks to correct misalignment and disconnection and to restore balance, grace, and flow. It is a function that is not unique to Christ, but it is a function that is also part of the nature of Christ: to do whatever is necessary to allow the "I" to be held in an unobstructed way within all levels and forms of incarnation and cosmos.

PERSONAL EMBODIMENT

Capacity and Identity

As a formative activity that is part of the structure of creation, Christ is not just something God does or is; it is something everything in creation does and is. Think of Christ as a natural function, like gravity. I exert a gravity field appropriate to my mass. The earth exerts a gravity field appropriate to its mass. In actual fact, the earth and I mutually attract, but the mass of the earth is so much greater than mine that the overall net effect is as if only the earth were attracting me, holding me in its gravity. Yet, we are both "attractors," both "holders."

There is what could be called analogously "metaphysical mass" or "consciousness mass" or "presence mass," as well. I have a certain amount of it through which my "I" expresses as an incarnate human being. A solar entity or an angel or a saint may have a good deal more of it than I, so its "I"-field, its expression of a Christos function may be much greater and more evident than my own, just as the gravity of the earth is more evident than my own. But this does not mean I am not also, expressing AS A SOURCE the function, activity, and presence of Christos.

This is the difference between Capacity and Identity. The universe is made up of infinite diverse manifestations of capacity. The capacity of an archangel to manifest sacredness may be very much more than my capacity to do so (though the comparison is not exact, since we are not of the same species and function in quite different realms), but we each can recognize, align with, attune to, hold and express our "I"-ness, our Identities as sacred beings.

As capacities, we differ. As identities, we are equal.

The capacity and function of Christ is as much in us—and always has been in us, even before the Christ event measured by the birth of Jesus—as anywhere else in creation. We may not have the same capacity to express it as other beings may have, but we cannot set a threshold and say, "Only that function of Christ which exceeds this threshold I have set can actually be called 'Christ.'"

Jesus loved and I can love. Jesus's love may have been planetary in scope, reflecting the love that flows continually from the "I", while I may only be able to love my dog (if I had one!) and that's the extent of my capacity. But is my love for my dog any less "Love" than Jesus's love for the world and all of life? Put another way, is the water in my glass any less wet than the water in the ocean?

Can I make a threshold and say, "only that love that embraces at a minimum one bioregion and all the lives within it and one million people as well counts as Love." At what point does my love become LOVE, the Love of the "I" expressed into the world? Is it when it embraces one person, twelve people, a hundred people, a million people?

You can see that this question makes no sense and is silly. It is a question that confuses capacity with identity. It confuses the presence of "I" with the expression of that "I."

The Christ of history is understood as a Christ that embraces the whole planet in its influence and love. But that is not a measure of Christ as function. Each of us also has the identity of and capacity for that function; each of us is also Christos and can express that function to the best of our ability. To say that to be Christ we must be as Jesus was is to misunderstand the nature of Christ and to separate ourselves from our own "I."

Being Christ as Redemption

With that in mind, how might we be to our own history, our own individual world, what the Christ of History was and is to the planet as a whole? How do we embody and express a redemptive function in our own personal life?

Remember that overall redemption is not a primary activity of Christ but a secondary activity that supports the primary function. The primary function is to connect with, hold and express the "I", the sacredness within us. The secondary function is to do whatever is necessary to enable that connection, holding, and expression to take place: to clear out the junk and to unkink the thread.

In the context of redemption, redemption means to reclaim and own our wholeness. It means to restore and realign any flow of spirit and life within us and in our relationships with the world that has become lost, kinked, stuck, misaligned, and so on.

Here are some examples.

My desk is so cluttered that I am continually distracted and do not have a good, steady flow of concentration and attunement with my work. I clean my desk up, reorganizing it, getting rid of stuff I don't need anymore, creating a clear, open space. In this action, I am performing an act of Christ to the degree that I am restoring flow and that flow gives expression to my creative presence. It enables me to align with my creative and inspirational "I", which may be the fullest form of my sacred "I" that I can currently recognize and to which I can attune.

****

I have had a spiff with a friend and carry anger in my heart and memory over this. This anger and the memories to which it is attached obstruct the flow of relationship and love between us. We become disconnected and misaligned with each other. To reclaim this friendship and its full flow of mutual love, inspiration, support, and co-creativity, I forgive my friend. I let the anger go. I try to experience the memories—the event that caused the anger—from my friend's point of view so my own perception and understanding can be enlarged. In so doing, I redeem this friendship, at least for myself, which is a huge start in redeeming it for both of us. This is a Christ function.

****

Gossip, complaints, misunderstanding, and ill-will all are affecting the environment in which I work. My co-workers and I do not get along, nor do we particularly wish to. As a result, going to work everyday is something I dread, something that enervates me. There is no inspirational, creative flow.

But one day, I decide to do something about this. Perhaps I bring flowers and begin to add some color and beauty to my workspace. I bring in a treat, like donuts, for everyone to share. I refuse to engage in gossip but deliberately seek out actions and behaviors in my co-workers that I can praise. I seek out ways I can appropriately support them in their work, ways that I can be encouraging and uplifting. I work on my own style of communication and make an extra effort to bring clarity into our group communication.

In short, I act to reclaim the potential co-creativity in our relationships and thus in our workplace. I may also, do inner work to shift the energies at work. Over time, the atmosphere in our workplace begins to change, becoming more open and cooperative. There is greater flow, and work is no longer the enervating experience that it was. I am redeeming my work and that of others who are my colleagues.

****

I am aware of stagnant and depressed energies in my environment. The inner atmosphere seems "smoggy". I center myself in a place of inner strength and calm, and invoke clarity, love, and gracefulness into my consciousness. I imagine myself surrounded by a clean, brisk open space, as if I were standing on a bluff overlooking the sea, with cleansing sea breezes blowing around me, filling my space with calm and freshness. I extend that presence of calm, freshness, grace, love, and power into my environment. I imagine the stagnant, depressed and even toxic energies being stirred up, as a broom stirs up dust as it sweeps the floor clean. I imagine my clean and clear presence filling the space around me, transmuting and removing the stagnant energies. I am blessing the space around me, and I ask for the space itself to join me in that blessing. Together we hold grace and clean energies. I am redeeming this space, restoring it to a state of alignment So, that there is a clean, clear flow of spirit through it and within it.

Awakening Christos
These actions I take in the examples above may not seem

like "Christ" to us. They may not seem sacramental or miraculous enough, nor do they in themselves necessarily put us in touch with our sacredness.

Part of that is that we are measuring our actions against a threshold of what constitutes Christ and what doesn't. We are engaging with capacity rather than with identity. We have an image of what a Christ-action is, or should be, or must be in order to qualify as being a Christ-action.

But Jesus, who is our primary model and threshold figure in this area, didn't just heal the sick, raise the dead, walk on water, and save the world. His Christness was not in miracles but in the ordinary things a person does as well. It existed in tone of voice, in kindness of words, in attentiveness in listening, in silent support and friendship, for all these things enhance flow and connection. When those are enhanced, even in very ordinary and seemingly trivial circumstances, the chances of connecting to and holding the presence of "I" is increased.

On the other hand, while Christ may not be measurable against a threshold of capacity, there can be a threshold of mindfulness, a threshold of the will to awaken and align. This is a threshold of self reaching for Self, of my everyday "I" reaching for the "I" at the core of my being and existence. It is the threshold of my personality deliberately and mindfully reaching for its sacredness.

This mindful reaching is also, a flow. It is a flow that awakens and expands Identity. I can do many "redemptive" things in my life, in my relationships, at work, and so on, all of which embody the essence of the Christ function (indeed it is the Christ function within me that ultimate allows me to do those things, that gives me the conscience and the love to wish to organize, forgive, be creative, and so on). I can be a truly loving fellow and still not become aware of any deeper sacredness or Identity or life within me. I can establish what I might call "local flow" and still be ignorant of or cut off from "cosmic flow."

The Christ is awakened in me as a consciousness and presence—and not only as a function—by my act of will for that awakening to happen. I am willing myself to be open and aware of my larger identity.

I don't have to do this in a religiously Christian way. This mindfulness transcends religion. I can do it as a Moslem, as a Jew, as a Buddhist, as a Wiccan, using whatever inspirational images work for me. Christ is more than a name, more than a belief. It is a living Identity and Presence of sacredness within all things. I can use the word "Christ" if I wish, or I can use another image, such as the "I", or my sacredness, or Mystery. But whatever I use, the point is that I perform my Christ function, such as the capacity for redeeming, with awareness that I am doing so as a link with and expression of that Christos that is my sacredness, my "I."

This can be a challenge, especially for Christians, for we have been taught to think of Christ in certain ways, So, being mindful of Christ can bring to mind all those cultural and religious images I asked you to list in Chapter One. If they are helpful, that's ok. But what I encourage you to strive for is a sense of ordinariness and naturalness about all this. Being Christ is like learning to breathe; it is an innate function that is perfectly natural and ordinary.

Looking back at the examples I gave, the "awakening Christ" aspect would be that in each instance I am aware that I am calling on and using a Christ function, and that the overall objective is to hold sacredness within myself and within my world, so that that sacredness is available in whatever way it is needed. It is to recognize an unbroken chain of being and Self from the "I" that is my sacredness to the "I" that is my sense of everyday self, or my personality.

Anytime I forgive, unblock, unobstruct, realign, reclaim, remember, recover, and redeem, I am performing the redemptive work of Christ. If I do so as an act of also recovering my sense of my "I" and thus redeeming my Identity, then I am awakening to Christ in my being, so that it becomes not just performance but presence as well. Identity opens to become capacity.

THE CHRIST EXERCISE: PART 1

EXERCISE 1

Light a candle. It represents the Christ of History, the Christ as Redeemer and Savior. It represents a specific field of energy within the World Soul that has been developing over the past two thousand plus years. As such, it contains a great many images that have been accumulated over this time. It is the traditional Christ of Christianity that millions of people have invoked, worshipped, called upon for help, for Light and Love, and have seen as a link to the Sacred. Yet, in your attunement, you want to go beyond the historical accumulations to the essence of this Christ field, this redemptive identity. Imagine what this energy and presence is like. Attune to its essence.

What does it mean to you? How do you experience it? How is it relevant to your life? How might it live in you? How might you become Christ Redeemer? What is Christ for you beyond redemption?

When you have completed your reflection, give thanks for any and all insights received and energies experienced. Then blow out your candle, bringing your awareness and focus gracefully back into your everyday life.

EXERCISE 2

I would like you during this time to be aware of how you express the Christ function through your own acts of realigning, unobstructing, recovering, forgiving, healing, cleansing, remembering, and redeeming.

What examples can you give of these actions?

Do they feel like Christ to you? If so, how and why? If not, why not?

As you do these kind of actions, remember that you do them as Christ. What does this feel like in you? What happens to you as you step into a Christ Identity?

Remember, Christ Identity is not to be confused with Christ Capacity. How do you experience this? What does this mean to you?

Spend this time being the Redemptive Christ and pay attention to what happens for you.

Chapter Four:
Jesus And The Christ Of Incarnation

THE CHRIST AND INCARNATION

In the last chapter, I suggested the Christos is the capacity within us to hold our sacredness, our "I". In a broad sense, it could be considered the capacity of the manifest cosmos to hold sacredness within itself, the capacity of the finite to hold the infinite.

However, this image can make the Christ seem passive, like a cup in which sacredness is stored or an altar where we go to find a link with God. The Christ is more than just connective tissue. The link with the sacred is one of being, and being is active. The "I" is not just held, it expresses. The fruits of its expression are creative manifestations: incarnations. Another way to say it is that what is held by Christ is not a thing but a creative, generative activity, and to hold an activity, the Christ itself is dynamic and active.

Christ is the mediator or "edge" of incarnation. Christ ensures that the Unmanifest and the Manifest, the Creator and the Created, the Sacred and the Cosmos, are not two things but are one wholeness in two forms. Christ is the manifestation of that innate wholeness. But Christ is also the activity of that wholeness within each side, so to speak, the presence of the Manifest within the Unmanifest, and the presence of the Unmanifest within the Manifest. It is the mediating presence that ensures that the capacity and presence of incarnation, manifestation, creativity, and sacredness is active throughout the realms of cosmos.

THE MYTHIC STORY, Part 2

In the beginning, St. John declares in his gospel, there was the Logos, the Word. And the Logos was with God, and the Logos was God. And Logos was Christ.

In the beginning, the Word was spoken and Creation came into being. But the Word, the Logos-Christ, was with Creation as well and was Creation. And in the midst of Creation, the Word was spoken again and yet again. With each speaking, new realms were born, new worlds emerged. Creation became Cosmos.

And now the Word was with Cosmos and the Word was Cosmos. And still it spoke, for a Word must be spoken and speaks itself.

The Word spoke and the world came into being. And the Word was with the world and was the world. And the world spoke itself as World, and there was Nature: plants and animals and human beings. And the Christ-Logos, the Word, was with plants and animals and human beings, and it was these things.

The Universe was filled with Speaking, and from the Word, new Words emerged. From Christos, new Christs emerged. And in this way, Creation and Cosmos unfolded and evolved, and the Unmanifest was made evident in the Manifest, the sacred in the world.

As the Word was spoken again and again, it grew in meaning and nuance. It gathered depth to itself. It was always spoken but never twice the same way, for each new voice gave it its own timbre, its own pitch, its own unique sound. It was the Word, but it was also Words. It was the Christ, but it was also Christs, always one, always emerging, always different, always the same.

The Word took flesh, and the Word was with flesh, and the Word was flesh. And as flesh multiplied, it remained the Word.

Humanity is a sacred idea, a cosmic presence. But on earth,

that presence unfolds in ways that are unique to this world. Cradled within the kingdoms of form, it begins to acquire the components of experience and consciousness that will coalesce and emerge as a human being.

In this process, there are vital stages when something new is added and something new unfolds. These may be thought of as initiations.

In the history of humanity, the first of these initiations was the seeding of the race into the earth itself, the response of a cosmic humanity to an upwelling of desire, intent, and power from the World Soul. This is the birth of humanity within the earth.

The second great initiation was the introduction and unfoldment of mind and intelligence within evolving humanity, separating it from its long gestation within the collective field of nature. It was at this point that humanity emerged from the animal kingdom. This could be called the initiation of the self, the gradual emergence first of a human collective self distinct from nature and then the emergence of individual human selves, distinct from the group.

The third great collective initiation was the initiation of sovereignty, the unfoldment of awareness of the sacred "I" within incarnation. The Christ Event is part of this initiation. It is also, the initiation of love, not the emotion of affection but the fiery presence, connectivity, and creative energy of the "I".

The fourth great collective initiation for Humanity I might call the initiation of Will. It is this initiation that is beginning now, and it offers the capacity to be a radiant and generative source of sacredness through a willed expression of the "I" and a will to support the presence of "I," the sacredness within all beings and within the world itself. It is the initiation of responsibility, the capacity to support, heighten, and energize the ability to respond to life as a sacred being. It gives expression and manifestation to the potential awakened by the Christ. It is the stage in which we are all Christs and the new name for Christ is simply "Person."

It is Humanity becoming and speaking the Word that brings a new coherency, harmony, and wholeness to the world.

THE MYTHIC STORY, Part 3

It is said that Jesus was overlighted and filled with the Christ, who in this context is seen as a radiant presence descending from higher spiritual worlds. There is truth to this, for any incarnation—and in particular one as attuned as that of Jesus—can be a portal through which the energies of the spiritual worlds can reach out to enter our own. In this case, such an overlighting may have been an important part of the redemptive work we discussed in our previous Mythic Story.

But to say that this is all that Jesus was, just a vessel or an instrument or a channel for another being or another force to work through, would not be true. Jesus is seen as son of God, a part of God, a sacred being in himself, and so are we all, for sacredness is in the substance and identity of us all.

In Jesus, though, we have not just the son of God but, as he styled himself, the son of Man. He was an emergent point of Christ arising from within humanity, from within the earth. He was not just heaven making a link with earth. He was the sacredness of the earth making a link with the sacredness of all things.

He was a Christ of earth, a Christ of humanity, embodying in a mindful way the sacred "I", the sacred Light innate within all incarnations. He made an unconscious, unseen, unknown sacredness conscious, seen, and real. He unveiled the Christos, giving it manifestation from the grass roots of our beings and the earth as well as from the heavens. He was the Christ of biology, chemistry, and physics, a Christ of matter as well as of spirit, even as we are.

FORMATIVE ACTIVITY

When we think of the Sacred, the image we most often use is that of Creator. We may think of a being like a potter, molding the universe out of some cosmic primordial substance.

But we could also, think of the Sacred as "Incarnator." The Cosmos becomes a form through which this presence may manifest, another way in which it may express its being.

An incarnation is certainly a manifestation. It is the taking on of a new form. But if that is all it is, then it is embodiment, not incarnation. Incarnation implies participation and engagement. It also implies emergence, the appearance of something that is more than what has gone before and more than the sum of its parts. Its characteristics may not be predictable from the characteristics of those parts or from what has gone before.

Consider an actor on a stage doing a play. Simply stepping onto the stage is not incarnation. It is embodiment. Incarnation is the engagement of the actor with the other actors, the audience, and the script and subject matter of the play itself. It is participation in the unfoldment of the drama that brings the story alive. It is also engagement and participation with the activity of Drama itself: the tradition of the stage, stagecraft, creativity, and so on. From this engagement and participation, the play emerges, and it will never be exactly the same each time it is performed. Each time the play is staged, something new emerges, if only because it is a new audience who will have new reactions.

At the same time, the presence of the actor and his or

her identity (both as an actor and as a character in the play) draws out and enhances the identities and presences of the other actors. He or she makes the set come alive. He or she draws something out from the audience. In short, identity fosters identity.

We all become more "real" or present when one person is being real and present.

Incarnation unfolds the deeper identity that is within all things. It reveals the "I". In this revelation of the "I", the link between Unmanifest and Manifest is also revealed. A wholeness is revealed. When we can fully grasp the nature of our incarnations and engage with our world, we discover that this embodied life does not separate us from our souls or our spirits but unites us and reveals us as a wholeness. My incarnation as David Spangler is not separate from my soul. Through the presence of the "I", I experience myself as a wholeness, not as a split being, though I am aware that the form and expression of David—organized as it is to be part of this world—is not identical to the form and expression of my soul—organized as it is to inhabit a different world.

This is like saying that the actor in the play can be both his or her character in the drama and himself as an actor. Indeed, as a person, he or she is more than just an actor, and he or she can experience that larger identity without losing their capacity to be a good actor.

We think of incarnation as simply taking on a form, taking on flesh as the word implies. But it is an activity and might be more properly understood as a "quickening." Incarnation is an energy event that quickens the realm in which it occurs.

When I incarnate, my energy—ultimately the energy of my "I"—now becomes available to the realm in which I incarnate. It adds to the energy of that realm. It quickens it.

Analogously, our actor, when he or she is engaged on

stage with the other actors, brings his or her energy to the play. The play is energized; the other actors are energized. The audience is energized. The whole proceeding is quickened.

This says little about the quality or depth of that quickening. There is a spectrum of quickening here that can run the gamut from simply adding additional energy to a system (making it more than what it was) to heightening the whole system's capacity to function and express (making it better than what it was). There are many ways we can participate in and engage with our world, and some ways will have a more profound, deepening, integrative, generative, and holistic effect.

What gives an incarnation its greatest power as an act of quickening is the presence of the "I" or the sacred within that incarnation. This "I" serves both the specificity of the incarnation and the world in which it takes place, and the unfoldment and revelation of the universal sacredness within that world.

In affect, incarnation serves incarnation. Each incarnation should make all incarnations easier and more attuned. Each incarnation, as a sacred act, should reveal the sacredness that is present in all things, the "I" revealing the "I".

So, where is the Christ in all this?

I suggested the Christ is the capacity to hold and express the "I", our innate sacredness. But the "I" is not passive, nor is the holding of it passive. Sacredness is an activity, and the primal nature of this activity is to incarnate: to manifest forms of expression and to quicken the energy of those forms so that emergence can take place and sacredness be revealed.

The sacred incarnates so it can be itself in a new form. I don't incarnate so I can be someone else. I incarnate so I can be my Self in expression, engaged with and participating in a particular environment.

We hold sacredness by being and doing sacredness. The Christ is the capacity within the cosmos to be and do sacredness. It is the expressive identity of God acting as and within creation: the Logos or Word was with God and was God. And as that "Word" is spoken, it becomes present with every manifestation that results from that primal creative, incarnational act.

In the Christian tradition, Christ is seen as God incarnating into human form as an act of transformational and redemptive solidarity with humanity. Jesus is understood in this context as a unique Person, God incarnate, and only Jesus has this distinction.

However, if I understand Christ as the activity within incarnation that maintains the continuity of "I" and sacredness—the activity that makes the Unmanifest and the Manifest a wholeness rather than two separate things—then the significance of Jesus lies not in being a unique incarnation of God but in being a demonstration that God is in incarnation—that God IS incarnation. Jesus reveals not that God incarnates once in him but that all incarnations are manifestations of the sacred—of the "I"—in an infinite variety of forms.

Jesus also demonstrates the quickening power of an incarnation that truly knows itself. By showing that all incarnation is sacred, it reveals to us the deeper power of an incarnation. We may call this love or will or presence, but over and over again, Jesus pointed out to us the serving, contributing nature of incarnation: that an incarnation can quicken and heighten the possibilities of all other incarnations around it, and indeed the possibilities of the world as a whole.

Our usual image of incarnation is that we incarnate downward: we enter a body, we enter the earth, we descend from heaven or the spirit realms, and so on. We talk about the will of the soul that initiates an incarnation.

But incarnation is an emergent phenomenon as well. It rises up out of systems as well as entering systems from outside them. Incarnations are really co-incarnational enterprises.

The actor enters the play from off-stage, from the wider dimension of his life as a person and as an actor. But on stage, there awaits for him a role, a character, that has arisen from the play itself. This character emerges from and exists within the play. In the incarnation of the performance, actor and role merge, and a character emerges.

How many Hamlets are there? There is only one written Hamlet existing on the pages of Shakespeare's script, but there are as many Hamlet characters as there have been actors to play the melancholy Dane, each actor bringing his own skill, interpretation, and life to the role. The Hamlet that results is not simply the creation of Shakespeare, nor the creation of the actor and director. It is co-created by all the participants in any particular staging of this play. Some contribute more to the end result than others, for sure, and some performances are more skilled, but Hamlet emerges from participatory engagement and quickening, not just from a single source.

In thinking of incarnation, Jesus, Christ, and kindred topics, we can be misled by our conception of "the single source," that is, that everything comes from a single point of origin.

In fact, everything comes from the interaction of multiple sources. Everything comes from the activity of interactive relationships. It is this activity that is the source, and it is this activity that is mediated and held by Christ. The presence of Christ quickens and heightens the co-creative, co-emergent, co-incarnational activities that make incarnation—ultimately, that make Cosmos—possible.

I interpret this presence as love, but it can be understood as other qualities as well, such as wisdom, intelligence, and will—the will-to-be, the will-to-become, the will-to-engage-and-connect. However we see it, it is the activity that makes incarnation possible.

This activity is not just present in the highest spiritual realms or in the Unmanifest or in heaven. It is present everywhere. It is an intrinsic part of the earth and of all beings upon the earth. And wherever this activity is, it seeks to unfold, improve, grow, evolve, and so on. It seeks quickening so that it may in turn quicken.

In the context of planetary and human evolution, this means that there is an "I" of the world and an "I" of humanity that seeks to unfold and express, that seeks to incarnate. There is a Christ within the earth, within humanity, that seeks unfoldment.

Previously, I said that here is a whole other Christ Act or Event that is not redemptive in nature *per se*. The heart of the Christ Act is not redemption but something else. That something else is the awareness of being and embodying sacredness. It is the awakening of our incarnational ability to quicken the expression of sacredness in ourselves and in our world. It is the awakening of our capacity to participate and engage mindfully in the co-creative, co-emergent, co-incarnational process that allows sacredness to be seen and expressed in our world.

It is the awakening of the capacity to hold sacredness in such a way that it becomes an active force within us, enabling us to hold and quicken it in the world as a whole. This capacity is present in all things, but it is not always active. Christ, like Lazarus, can sleep in a tomb of unconsciousness and unawareness, waiting to be called forth. Jesus called it forth in a particularly powerful way. He said, What I am, you can be; what I do, you can do also, and greater things besides.

He was an incarnation of quickening.

Jesus, to me, embodied the Christ emerging from the world, the "Bio-Christ." He was, as he said, the son of man, the product of humanity and of this world. He was, as we all are, the sacred AS incarnation, which permitted, in his case, a specific manifestation of the sacred IN incarnation.

I have a final thought here.

The Bible affirms that God so loved the world that He gave his only begotten son for our benefit. But this is true for all of us. We also, can say, "We so love the world that we give ourselves, in our sacredness, that the world may be quickened and the sacred made accessible."

PERSONAL EMBODIMENT

The very fact that we are incarnate beings IS the personal embodiment of this aspect of Christos.

This is true whatever the form of that embodiment. I, as a physical being, am still the activity and identity of sacredness—of Christ—just as much as if I did not have a physical body. And I can look about me at the world and in all the things I see—the animals, the plants, the other people—I am also looking upon the activity of Christ as incarnation.

Remember that incarnation is not simply an act or an event. It is an ever-emergent process of engagement and connection. I have an incarnation because I am involved with the world, not simply because I am here. This involvement may be very minimal or it may be very active and wide-ranging, but it is still there. I am not inert!

The activity of Christ lives in that engagement, in the activity of being present—and being a presence.

Responsibility

Responsibility often carries a sense of duty and obligation, and it can be used as a synonym with accountability. But I would suggest an alternative perspective on this word. "Responsibility" to me means literally the capacity to respond, to be engaged, to be aware. It means to me being a participant.

When I am responsible for someone or something, it means I am alive to them, present to them, aware of them and their situation, and willing and able to respond, particularly in ways that enhance their wellbeing. I am a participant in the energy that flows between us and around us.

Of course, there are many ways to respond and participate. What makes a particular response truly incarnational and Christic is when it quickens the other energetically and heightens or enhances their capacities to incarnate more gracefully, fully, and creatively themselves.

Co-Incarnation

This becomes clearer when we consider the idea of co-incarnation, the ways in which we enhance each other's being and incarnations. When we think about incarnation, it can be as if all the motive and power and energy is coming from a singular source. We are incarnations of our souls, we say, and look to our souls as the sources of our earthly lives. But in fact, who and what we are also emerges out of our various relationships and connections here on the earth. My soul is not the only voice determining who I am; other voices chime in, too. Incarnation becomes a cooperative venture.

Since every bit of creation bears the incarnating "I"—the will of the Unmanifest to be Manifest—then every such bit begins to do what the "I" does: incarnate, manifest, create, emerge, and unfold. Each "I" is a source for further incarnation. Each manifestation of "I" is the edge where the Unmanifest becomes the Manifest and creation emerges into being.

All these bits of "I"—all these "I-Fractals""—recognize each other and support each other. How could they not? They are in essence the same Presence. They blend wills. They vibrate and resonate to the joyous acts of becoming and manifesting. In this process, incarnation becomes co-incarnation, creation becomes co-creation, manifestation becomes co-manifestation, and emergence becomes co-emergence. The cosmos unfolds from all this activity of relationship.

I can further illustrate this with my metaphor of the actor in the play. An actor can co-create a play with other actors simply by reciting his lines, answering his cues, and engaging with his compatriots on stage. He can do the minimal amount of connecting, communicating, and engaging necessary to perform the play.

But when an actor goes into his depth and draws on his love for theater, his love of his craft, his identity as an actor, and makes all that available on stage in his role, AND when he expresses this as a support to encourage and enable his fellow actors to do their best and to be the best actors they can be, so that the play is not just performed but lived, quickened, heightened, and expanded, then the audience sees something very special. A wonderful co-generative energy is released.

The activity of Christos is not just connecting. It is connecting in a way that recognizes, affirms, reaches out to, and supports the "I" in another…quickening the capacity of that other to fulfill the will and spirit inherent in its incarnation, to be all that it can be.

This is responsibility: enhancing the capacity within oneself, within others, within a situation, to respond to the incarnational potentials and the presence of the sacred that are inherent all around us.

Co-incarnation proceeds by responsibility. When that responsibility is to the life and manifestation of the "I" within all things, then that responsibility is an expression of Christ.

To embody the activity of Christos as incarnation, we look to those opportunities to enhance, bless, and quicken the lives of the beings around us, human and non-human. And the energy that performs this function powerfully and well is that of love.

We come, then, to what has always been seen as the embodiment of Christ: the ability to love.

EXERCISE ONE:

In this exercise pay attention to the different things you do as an incarnate person: walking, driving, eating, talking, resting, working, and so on. Imagine Jesus doing these things. Imagine yourself as Christ doing these things. Reflect on how these common, everyday activities may evoke love, compassion, and Christ-ness from you. Reflect on how they connect you to all of humanity, to the earth, to nature, to the land, to the city, and so forth, and how through those connections, your own spacious spirit, your own light and sacredness may flow. Reflect on yourself as a Christ—the loving spirit, the connective spirit, the spacious spirit— in incarnation.

Which of your activities seem to most evoke a sense of the Christ in you? Why might this be so? When is it easiest for you to see yourself as an incarnate Christ? When is it most difficult?

EXERCISE TWO:

Do you see your life as having the capacity to quicken

the energy, potentials, and life of others around you? That is, are there ways in which you make it more possible for others to be themselves and to unfold their "I"? What might these ways be?

In this exercise, reflect on yourself and your incarnation as a source of quickening.

THE CHRIST EXERCISE: Part 2

Light a second candle. The first candle represented the Christ of History, the Christ as Redeemer and Savior. This second candle represents the Christ of Incarnation, as represented by Jesus, the Christ in human incarnation.

This image invites you to meditate upon the divinely human, the humanly divine. Please focus beyond any and all religious and mystical accumulations around the Christ and attune to this Presence as a human being. Jesus is a person like yourself who found his inner Christos within his humanness, within his biology and chemistry and earthiness, within his flesh and heart, mind and soul, within his family and his relatedness, within his attunement to the world soul and to the earth as a creature of this planet. Here you are attuning to a person who was once just like you and did what you are now seeking to do. Imagine what his energy and presence are like, attune to their essence, and invoke it into your awareness. Then imagine yourself as an incarnate Christ. What does this feel like?

Life itself is the great "exercise" we're all involved with, and it contains plenty of stimulation and openings to inspire our spirit to connect with the Christ, or just with sacredness in general. The challenge from my point of view is that we believe that Christ and the Sacred are external realities, beings and qualities that are "out there." As a consequence, we miss opportunities that life does present to experience the quality of Christ or the Sacred as an interior reality and part of who we are. Really, all you need do is to affirm to yourself, "I open my heart to Christ within my world and within myself, knowing that its presence and expression is a natural and organic part of who I am."

Chapter Five:
The Cosmic Christ

THE MYTHIC STORY

Jesus represents a very particular manifestation and incarnation of Christ. Unfortunately, over the centuries Christianity has come to see him as the primary, even the only, manifestation of Christ.

But the Christ is much larger than Jesus. Even if we take Jesus to be the divine Son of God or a form of God itself, he is still only one of many possible forms, one of many sons and daughters of the sacred. Jesus then becomes a message from a God separate from creation, rather than a participant with us in the presence and beingness of the sacred within creation. Isolating Jesus from his humanity and isolating Christ within Jesus is to deny the co-creative, co-generative presence of Christ within us all. It denies the very essence of what Christ is, turning it simply into an interface between God and humanity.

There has always been a faction within Christianity—usually its mystics—who have known that Christ is more than that. They perceived that Christ is a mystery and a presence beyond the incarnation of Jesus. They saw that Christ was not just an earthly manifestation but a cosmic one as well. And as such it linked humanity and the earth with the vastness of God's cosmos.

In some esoteric Christologies, the Christ is understood as a Solar being—an entity associated with the Solar Logos and operating from that level of intensity and spirit—who overlighted Jesus and anchored an initiatic solar energy within the earth. In effect, he anchored within the earth the love and spirit that operates within the Solar realm as an act of quickening and of redemption, making that level of spirit and energy accessible to human beings in ways that had previously only been accessible to a few highly trained and developed adepts.

In this context, the Cosmic Christ could be seen as the next level up, bringing to earth—not through an individual but through humanity itself as a collective being—the energies and spirit that operate at a Stellar level, making them available to an increasing number of individuals who, by embodying those energies, can make them available to the earth. The approach of this being stimulates the minds and hearts of human beings, giving birth to ideas that can resonate with the stellar energies and teachings now entering the earth's field.

The ideas that are being stimulated are those that move us from solar models of organization and structure (the primacy of a center, the dominance of a single source, the structure of a single leader, guru, or teacher around whom others orbit like planets and receive teachings and energy). In their place come ideas of holism, synthesis, synergy, co-creativity, systems, ecology, and the like. These are ideas that reflect the metaphor of the galaxy as a condition in which there are many stars, each of whom is a source of radiance, in relationship with each other, rather than the metaphor of the solar system in which a single radiant source, the sun, dominates and gives energy to planets who are essentially passive receivers.

It could also be said that humanity, in the course of its evolution and development, and in response to the work of Jesus and others in heightening a consciousness of sacredness, has touched into its own cosmic nature, its own expansive capacities. As before, the Cosmic Christ is not simply a being or a force that is coming to us from outside but a realization, an expansion, a consciousness arising from within us. As humanity begins to see itself in a cosmic context, a vision much heightened by modern technology and space travel, it begins to open to the possibilities that our consciousness and spirit may inhabit and engage with—incarnate into—the cosmos in new and unprecedented ways.

FORMATIVE ACTIVITY

When incarnation occurs, a form emerges. This form has something that acts as a boundary, however permeable it may be, and it has an internal consistency. The boundary provides definition but it also provides limits. The internal consistency creates the structure for an identity, a unique foundation upon which the "I" may emerge and express.

Both boundaries and identities can become closed and limited in ways that become inappropriate in that they generate a sense of closure for the system's development and growth.

I may, for instance, say that the material world is all there is and that any suggestion that I have powers of mind or spirit that can affect the world is nonsense. I close myself off to those possibilities and capacities.

The particle can deny the wave.

But the "I" is neither particle nor wave, neither particular nor universal. The Sacred by its nature encompasses both extremes and all in between. To deny one or the other is to limit the horizon of our possibilities, the fullness of our incarnations.

Therefore, the process of incarnation includes that which is "meta" or "other" to the form and system of that incarnation. Each system is challenged not to become wholly closed (though it may appropriately in a given situation become relatively closed or fixed, like the rocks that channel the flow of a river) but to come to the edge of its form and being and see what possibilities lie beyond.

This calling to the edge—and the capacity to stand at the edge and look over and beyond the boundary and identity of an incarnation in order to open to newness and possibility—is also an expression of the Christ. It is an activity represented by the image of the Cosmic Christ.

The experience of the Cosmic Christ is often understood in contrast to the image of Jesus Christ. Jesus is perceived by many Christians as the identity and boundary of Christ; that is, Jesus was the Christ, the Son of God, the Incarnate Sacred, and no one else can be.

Mystics and spiritual seekers have gone to the "edge of Jesus" and seen that beyond this particular Christic manifestation is a universal Christ, the Christ consciousness or principle, as well as, in some traditions, a cosmic presence that embodies Christ much as Jesus embodied it for our world. This opens new and exciting possibilities for our experience of Christ. We may not be able to become Jesus, but we can become the Christ Consciousness and Presence. The Cosmic Christ is open to all of us.

The Cosmic Christ embodies that function that acts as a horizon, drawing us beyond what is simply familiar and routine and towards new possibilities. It opens us up. It takes us beyond the specificity of a particular incarnation, with its defining boundaries and limits, and invites us to revision who we are. It lifts us beyond the particular and into the universal. More precisely, it allows us to see ourselves as being both particle and wave, both the particular and the universal.

In the Cosmic Christ, we encounter Christ as a principle or as a state of consciousness. In the Redemptive Christ, we have the Christ as an activity. In the Incarnate Christ, we have Christ as a presence to whom we may relate and which enables us to see the Christic possibilities both in our incarnations and in incarnation as a sacred activity. In the Cosmic Christ we open to the possibilities of identity, of sharing and participating in a principle or consciousness ourselves. We can see that we, too, can be this presence, that it is not exclusive to a particular incarnation or person.

This is an act of recognition and expansion as much as an act of revelation. That is to say, there is an activity in us that allows us to extend beyond our particularity, that allows us to be "cosmic." The Cosmic Christ—the presence of the universal—could stand before me and tell me all day that I, too, am a universal being and that I, too, am a Christ. But if I am unable to find it in me to see beyond my specificity and particularity—beyond my boundaries of consciousness as an incarnate individual—I may not and probably will not be able to respond.

The Cosmic Christ is not simply a larger dimension or version of Christ existing beyond the world in some domain of universality. It is a capacity for growth and expansion within ourselves. It is a capacity, arising from our own "I", our own root sacredness, to see that we, too, are part of that universality. It is a capacity to find in ourselves an identity that is part of our incarnation but not confined to it

Cosmic Christ, Universal Christ, Christ Consciousness, the Christ Principle...these are all terms we can use to indicate not only a Christic presence beyond us—and beyond the specific incarnation of Jesus—but our own capacity to identify with the universal and with a whole larger than our particular selves.

It is that capacity, that inner function and activity, that allows us to step beyond our specific selves and enter the life of another, to walk in another's shoes. It is the capacity that negates selfishness and our tendency to define ourselves solely by our own limits and boundaries. In that sense, it is a capacity for love, but then love is at the root of the "I" in any event and at the heart of all manifestations of Christ. But even more, it is the capacity for an expanded identity that can contain and honor but not be limited by our own particularity.

PERSONAL EMBODIMENT

The Cosmic Christ or the universal Christ Principle is a presence whom I may encounter in any being that seeks to awaken and engage with my own innate sacredness and draw me beyond my own perceived and accepted limits and definitions.

As an activity within me, I find it in those mental, emotional, and physical acts that take me to the edge of my incarnation, the edge of my familiarity, and open me to new possibilities of identity and beingness.

I find it as well in those acts that expand my sense of identity beyond my own boundaries to include and connect with others. It is what takes me beyond any particular self-image and enables me to participate in a larger wholeness. It enables me to experience another as myself.

It is the act of discovering and embodying my own innate universality. It is the activity of being "cosmic."

"Cosmic" is a word usually used in quantitative ways to denote something that is very large. But it can be used qualitatively to suggest a perspective and a consciousness that is inclusive and expansive. It is a consciousness that is not so much limitless in the sense of not recognizing any limits but one that redefines limits so they can be tools of definition but not obstructions to beingness, communion, and communication. Boundaries and limits support identities, but they are also the jumping off points for an expansion of identities.

In the old classic Star Trek TV show, the mission of the

Enterprise was to seek out new worlds, new civilizations, and to boldly go where no one had gone before. It was a cosmic mission. But we have the same mission. We are surrounded by new and unexplored worlds in the guise of all the people who surround us. How do we engage with them? How do we appreciate and enter into their worlds, their unique perspectives? How do we boldly go where we have not gone before, into the unexplored territory of another's heart and mind? Our capacity to do this, to reach through love and attention beyond ourselves, to be open to another as well as to new potentials within ourselves (our own unexplored territories and inner "new worlds") is our capacity to be "cosmic."

We might look upon this activity as the capacity to learn and thus to grow. But it is more than just that. Learning and growth can be linear and predictable. The activity of the Cosmic Christ is to stand at that open edge where transformation and true newness can happen, where the learning is not predictable or linear. How do we open ourselves to that kind of edge in our lives?

Considering that each of us can be a Christ, that the Christ is not always something beyond us or other than us, can be such an edge. We open to a new horizon, a new possibility. Something within that larger identity can then respond. By discovering and touching our own capacity to be cosmic, we open an inner space for the cosmic to enter and be part of us.

Our capacity to imagine can be an activity reflecting our inner "cosmic-ness." We can imagine ourselves in another's shoes. We can imagine ourselves going beyond our boundaries. We can imagine ourselves embodying "Christ-ness."

The Cosmic Christ is what transforms a boundary into a portal. What activities do we do that transform our boundaries into portals through which we can move into a larger, more inclusive, more expanded state?

EXERCISE ONE

Pay attention to horizons that call you beyond your limits. Pay attention to events and forces that uplift you, widen you, bring you into greater spaciousness. Pay attention to how you discover or create space in your life. Pay attention to how you discover and create openness in your life. In what ways do you enhance your inclusiveness and your expansiveness?

THE CHRIST EXERCISE: PART 3

Light a third candle. This represents the Christ as Principle, the Universal Christ transcending any particular religion or incarnation, the Cosmic Christ. What does this mean to you? What is your sense of "Cosmic"? How does Cosmic relate to the Christ for you?

Let yourself open to the Cosmic, to the horizon of potentials and possibilities. Become a Cosmic Being yourself. What is that like? What does it feel like within you and around you?

Imagine going to your own edge. What is that edge for you? What is the edge of your potentials, your possibilities, your incarnation, your self-definition? What new you lies beyond that edge? How might you expand into it?

Imagine a spacious spirit within you, one that is able to embrace and allow the differences of others. Imagine yourself as a core of spaciousness for your world around you. In this spaciousness, you and all around you have an opportunity to experience your innate universality and sacredness. What does this feel like to you?

Chapter Six:
The Emerging Christ

In this chapter, rather than using the previous format for the text (Mythic Story, Formative Activity, Personal Embodiment), I'm just going to hold forth on the theme of the emerging Christ and present the fourth part of the exercise. This will be followed by the final complete exercise.

I have been defining the Christ as that function in creation that connects the Unmanifest with the Manifest. It holds and maintains the identity of sacredness throughout all the myriad forms and dimensions of incarnation and being that make up the cosmos. In this sense, it is analogous to that function in us that links all the aspects of our incarnate self to our soul, giving us a coherent identity.

By holding the "I" of creation, this Christ function allows the sacred to explore incarnation through an infinity of forms and not lose itself. It keeps the "big bang" from being merely an explosion of rapidly separating parts in the cosmos. It allows creation to be a wholeness that is experiencing as well continual diversification and infinite variety. Christ is that sacred activity that makes possible the paradox of One Identity that can be both one and many, single and scattered, unified and diverse, at the same time.

This activity occurs at every level of creation, from the highest spiritual plane or the most extensive cosmic consciousness to the most condensed form of matter and the most limited and narrowly focused consciousness. This activity may look in form different depending on where and how it is taking place. The Christ function that acts in me to clear my desk and open a space through which I have a greater chance to connect with my "I" in the moment and to be creative is the same in function but very different in appearance, form, structure, expression, and consequences from the Christ that manifests as an avatar to bless and serve an entire planet. Still, for all their difference, these two acts share a resonance. Along the vibration of that resonance, I can be assisted in remembering and discovering the Christ in me.

How the activity of Christ actually manifests at any given time or in any given situation depends on what is necessary to remember the one in the many and the many in the one. What is necessary to manifest the sacred in creation and the sacredness of creation?

The answer to this in one situation may be some act of redemption or realignment; in another situation it may be some act of illumination and blessing; it may be a specific act of incarnation within a particular realm; it may be drawing the habits and routines of a system to its edge and opening up new possibilities.

It can also be through acts of emergence in which something unpredictable and unprecedented occurs and something new appears.

This is truly the Christ of Mystery. Who can say what it will be? When I was a child, I thought of Christ strictly in terms of Jesus. Jesus was Christ to me and vice versa. As I grew older, though, and began to have more spiritual experiences, another form of Christ began to emerge for me. Note that this other form was not in itself new—many people had experienced it—but it was new and emergent for me. And that was the idea of Christ as a spirit without form, as a presence that could enter into me and become part of me.

Still later, from this experience emerged another, the experience of Christ as an essential part of myself, which is to say the realization that Christ was not simply a force outside of me but one that was innate within me. And from this there later emerged the experience of Christ not simply as a spiritual aspect of my being but as part of the very substance, molecules, and atoms of my physical life: Christ as chemistry, Christ as physics.

Who knows what experience of Christ may emerge next?

We all go through these kind of changes, and they are more than just changes in belief or cosmology. They become reorganizations of our very mode and style of incarnation. They change who we are, not just what we think or believe.

Others throughout history almost certainly have experienced the different and expanded aspects of Christ that I have—and gone more deeply and further in understanding and embodying them than I have done—but this does not make them any less emergent for me. Emergence is a function in which any system transforms into a new form or relates with others to produce something unprecedented and unpredicted. As such, it is a singular event for that system or those systems. When life emerged on earth, it was a momentous occurrence, a holy event; never mind that life has emerged elsewhere as well.

This is because each act of emergence is unique since emergence is always related to a particular set of conditions. Each act of emergence is the sacred discovering something new about itself within a particular set of incarnational conditions.

Thus, even though thousands of people may have experienced the sense of a universal Christ consciousness before I did, when I experienced it, it was a unique emergence. In a sense, God had never experienced itself in that way before, because the incarnate self that is David Spangler had not existed before and had not had that emergent experience of Christ before—even though the remembrance of an incarnate being of its sacred identity—its Christos—has been going on on all levels of life since creation itself first emerged.

We might look upon creation itself as an emergent form of sacredness.

Though it may be strange to think of it this way, assuming such a thing were possible, had anyone been able to gaze upon the Unmanifest, would they have been able to predict that it would also become Manifest? Is Manifestation a natural and predictable expression of Unmanifestation? Or is Manifestation—the Manifest universe—an unpredictable, unprecedented emergent state of the Unmanifest?

Unanswerable questions, of course. Stimulating to think about, though!

My point is that emergence—becoming something new—is apparently a part of what the sacred is and does. It is a sacred activity and one of the ways in which the identity of the sacred manifests. Hence, emergence becomes one of the ways to hold, connect with, demonstrate, and remember the sacred within creation and thus an aspect of the Christ. "Behold, I make all things new."

At the very least, emergence reminds us that life and creation are in flux and that they are engaged in activity, motion, unfoldment, development, surprise, discovery, all of which become a link—a Christic activity—with the sacred.

Why?

Consider how the infinite becomes known through the finite. How many galaxies, stars, and planets must there be in order to reveal all the possibilities inherent in the sacred? A million galaxies? A billion? A quadrillion? How much finiteness equals infinity? The answer, of course, is that the finite realm, no matter how large, cannot equal infinity. There are never enough different galaxies to fully exhaust or reveal the sacred or the Unmanifest.

Emergence is not simply a function of growth or evolution. It is a way in which the sacred reveals itself because no prior revelation or incarnation has been sufficient to show all that the sacred is. It is a way the sacred demonstrates its identity within creation, and as such, it is a Christic activity, for it fulfills the function of Christ as that which ensures, promotes, reveals, and establishes the identity of the sacred within the cosmos.

Emergence itself may be seen as part of the Christ function, one of the ways that function is fulfilled. It is or can be a Christic activity.

By the same token, the nature and experience of Christ is emergent. The coming of Jesus and the incarnation of Christ is considered in the Christian tradition as a unique revelation of God. St. John writes that before Jesus incarnated, there was the Christ, that indeed the Christ had been present from the beginning of creation. But Jesus revealed a new form—an emergent form—of that Christ as "God-Man," God incarnate.

Are there new forms or understandings of Christ emerging in our time? Will such new forms emerge in the future?

How can we doubt it? It is the nature of Christ to both foster emergence and to be emergent in its own right.

So, in this fourth aspect of Christ, after looking at three known or familiar forms of Christ (Christ as redeemer, Christ as incarnated in Jesus, and the Cosmic Christ, the Christ principle within all things), we look at the Christ that cannot be predicted, the Christ of Mystery, the Christ that is emerging—always emerging—within ourselves, within our world, and within the cosmos.

THE CHRIST EXERCISE: Part 4

Light a fourth candle. This represents the Christ as Mystery, the Unknown Christ, the Emerging Christ who cannot be defined or held in any particular image. It is all the aspects and dimensions of Christ that cannot be contained by our images of the Christ of History, Jesus the Christ, or the Cosmic Christ. It is Christ as the undiscovered country, as the unknown Other, as the yet-to-be-revealed. Attune to this and see what images arise and, more importantly, what felt sense and empowerment arises in you. This is Mystery. How do you invite Mystery into your life?

Think of Christ as a Pathmaker between the known and the unknown, the familiar and the mysterious, the manifest and the potential, the past and the future. Reflect on Christ as a power of emergence. "Behold," Christ says, "I make all things new." How does this capacity unfold in your life? Where is the edge of newness, the edge of emergence, in your life? How do you stand at that place?

THE COMPLETE CHRIST EXERCISE

This is the final exercise, putting together all that we've covered in this book and adding the final bits that focus them within ourselves. The object of this exercise is simply to have an experience of the Christ within us, the Christ as us, and ourselves as Christic beings. It is an exercise in unveiling Christos.

This experience and the felt sense of it then becomes a foundation for growing more deeply into the presence and experience of Christ as a shared and universal principle. It is also, a foundation for growing into a deepening felt sense of your own "I", your own sacredness, and allowing that sacredness to act transformatively in your life and as a blessing to others.

The full Christ Exercise may be done as individual meditations, each focusing on one of the five elements described below. Or it can be done as a full ritual. When you are doing the latter, you will use six candles. You will arrange the first four candles in a circle around yourself, one at each of the cardinal directions of East, South, West, and North. The final two candles you will place within the circle.

Here is a diagram:

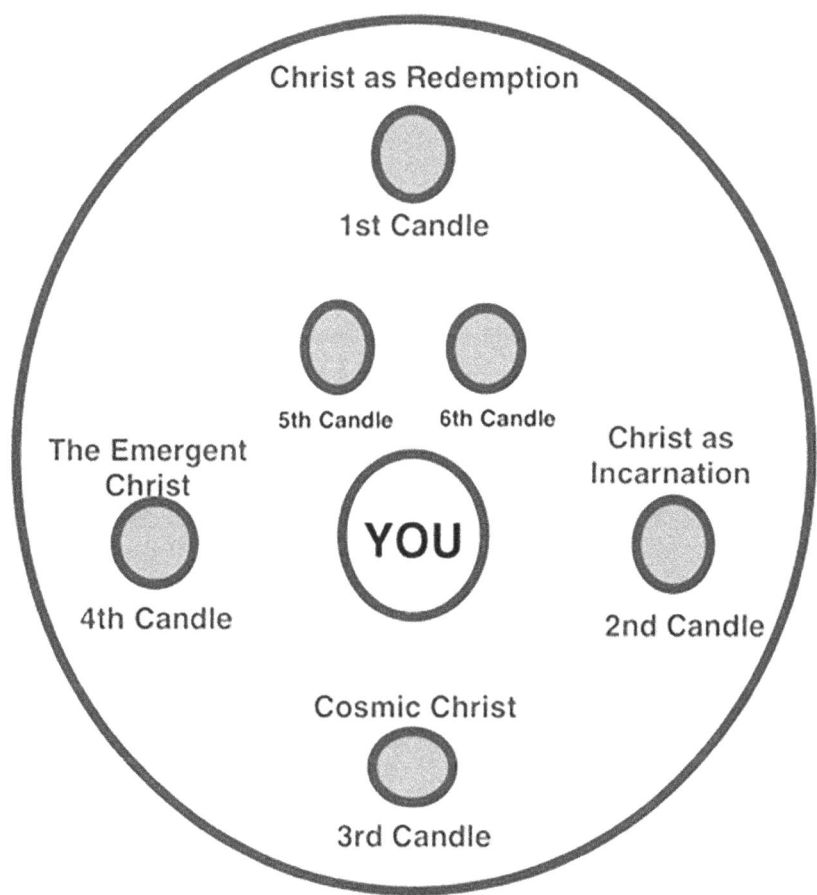

Enter the circle and face one of the candles. Light this candle and meditate upon it as described below. Then, moving in a clockwise manner, light each of the other three candles in turn, then the candles in the middle. (NOTE: This exercise involves lighted candles, so be aware of your surroundings. When dealing with open flames, you want to be aware of any possible danger and of anything that might catch on fire. Exercise skill and carefulness in doing this exercise.)

THE FIRST CANDLE

Light a candle. It represents the Christ of History, the Christ as Redeemer and Savior. It represents a specific field of energy within the World Soul that has been developing over the past two thousand plus years. As such, it contains a great many images that have been accumulated over this time. It is the traditional Christ of Christianity that millions of people have invoked, worshipped, called upon for help, for Light and Love, and have seen as a link to the Sacred. Yet, in your attunement, you want to go beyond the historical accumulations to the essence of this Christ field, this redemptive identity. Imagine what this energy and presence is like. Attune to its essence.

What does it mean to you? How do you experience it? How is it relevant to your life? How might it live in you? What in your life may need reclaiming, reowning, reordering, realigning? How might you become Christ Redeemer? What is Christ for you beyond redemption?

THE SECOND CANDLE

Light a second candle. This candle represents Jesus, the Christ, in human incarnation. This image invites you to meditate upon the divinely human, the humanly divine. Please focus beyond any and all religious and mystical accumulations around the Christ and attune to this Presence as a human being. Jesus is a person like yourself who found his inner Christ-ness within his humanness, within his biology and chemistry and earthiness, within his flesh and heart, mind and soul, within his family-ness and his relatedness, within his attunement to the world soul and to the earth as a creature of this planet. Here you are attuning to a person who was once just like you and did what you are now seeking to do. Imagine what his energy and presence is like, attune to its essence, and invoke it into your awareness. Then imagine yourself as an incarnate Christ. What does this feel like?

THE THIRD CANDLE

Light a third candle. This represents the Christ as Principle, the Universal Christ transcending any particular religion or incarnation, the Cosmic Christ. What does this mean to you? What is your sense of "Cosmic"? How does Cosmic relate to the Christ for you?

Let yourself open to the Cosmic, to the horizon of potentials and possibilities. Become a Cosmic Being yourself. What is that like? What does it feel like within you and around you?

Imagine going to your own edge. What is that edge for you? What is the edge of your potentials, your possibilities, your incarnation, your self-definition? What new you lies beyond that edge?

How might you expand into it?

Imagine a spacious spirit within you, one that is able to embrace and allow the differences of others. Imagine yourself as a core of spaciousness for your world around you. In this spaciousness, you and all around you have an opportunity to experience your innate universality and sacredness. What does this feel like to you?

THE FOURTH CANDLE

Light a fourth candle. This represents the Christ as Mystery, the Unknown Christ, the Emerging Christ who cannot be defined or held in any particular image. It is all the aspects and dimensions of Christ that cannot be contained by our images of the Christ of History, Jesus the Christ, or the Cosmic Christ. It is Christ as the undiscovered country, as the unknown Other, as the yet-to-be-revealed. Attune to this and see what images arise and, more importantly, what felt sense and empowerment arises in you. This is Mystery. How do you invite Mystery into your life?

Think of Christ as a Pathmaker between the known and the unknown, the familiar and the mysterious, the manifest and the potential, the past and the future. Reflect on Christ as a power of emergence. "Behold," Christ says, "I make all things new." How does this capacity unfold in your life? Where is the edge of newness, the edge of emergence, in your life? How do you stand at that place?

THE FIFTH CANDLE

Light the fifth candle in front of you.

This represents the Christ at the heart of your incarnation, the Christ that lives within you and helps facilitate your Deed of Incarnation. This is the Christ Spirit at the heart of you, the gift of the Sacred to you at the moment of your creation. This Christ quality is very specific to you; though it is part of a universal presence, it is uniquely configured to your soul and to you. Imagine what this energy and presence is like, attune to its essence, and invoke it into your circle.

THE SIXTH CANDLE

Now light the sixth candle. This represents the Christ you wish to become and be for the world. Invoke it through your name (I would, for example, invoke it as "David the Christ" or "David Christ" or "Christ David,"). Like the Christ of Mystery, it is unformed and without clear definition. Leave it that way. Don't try to define it or anticipate what it will or could be like. Just understand that it is the Christ presence that incarnates through you and as you in a unique way. Where the Christ within you, represented by the fifth candle, is the Christ at your foundation and at your "past," this is the Christ of your future, the Christ of your unfoldment, the Christ of You given in service and love and power to the world: "For I so love this world that I give myself to it in incarnation that it may know love and the Light of the Sacred and be liberated from all harm and all suffering!" Imagine what this energy and presence is like, attune to its essence, and invoke it into your circle.

UNVEILING CHRISTOS

At this point, you are in a circle with six candles lit, four around you at the cardinal directions of East, South, West, and North, and two in front of you.

Imagine a circle of Light and Presence around each candle, each representing the particular aspect of Christ you invoked: The Redemptive, Uplifting Christ of History; the Christ of the Jesus Incarnation, your elder brother; the Cosmic Christ as a universal principle; the Christ of Mystery, the Unknown Christ; the Christ at your foundation empowering and ensouling your Deed of Incarnation and Self; and the Christ you can become and will become, the emerging Christos of your unique incarnation.

Now pay attention to yourself at the center. Honor and uplift yourself in your thoughts and feelings. Know you are loved. Know you are worthy. Know you are a Grail that can contain the Christ.

Appreciate for a moment your incarnateness, your embodiedness, your selfness, your personhood, your uniqueness, just as you are with all your strengths and weaknesses, all your virtues and faults. Then see yourself as part of a great continuum of being stretching from the Sacred to the Earth and from the past to the future. You are part of an ecology of loving beings whose intent is to bring Light, Love, Wisdom, and a Co-creative Power to the earth that the Presence of the sacred may be known and manifested and blessings abundantly shared. Honor yourself and this ecology of being. Recognize and celebrate your uniqueness, your value, your presence, the particular gift of soul and contribution that you as a specific manifestation of the Infinite can bring to that ecology and to the earth itself.

This is your Christos. Unveil it!

Then, from each of these circles of Light and Presence, see a line of power, presence, light, love, and essence emerging and flowing into you and around you so that you sit in a column of presence, a bath of light filled with the essence of Christ. As a grail, you are filled with this unified essence and presence; it flows to all parts of your life and your soul's ecology of being and incarnation.

Pay particular attention to the quality and sensation, the feel and presence of this unified column of Christ-ness as it enfolds you and soaks into you.

Just be present to that unified Presence; just float in that bath. Don't try to visualize it doing anything in particular, but breath it in, soak it in. Let it call to and draw forth your own unique experience of Christ-ness. Be aware of any sensations, energies, ideas, images, visions, etc., which may arise. Commit yourself to remembering them (but don't strain to do so, just ask that you may remember all that is important), but don't try to analyze them. Just relax and soak. If you want to use a mantra to help you, say "I give myself to Christ as Christ gives itself to me. I draw the Christ into myself as myself. Let it flow from myself as myself. Let my Christos be unveiled in service and blessing to my world!"

Sit in this column of Christ Presence as long as you wish. But when you feel restless or your mind and heart begin to wander, then stop. Let yourself gracefully come into your body, your mind, your heart, your everyday personality. Feel how these aspects of you are held and hallowed by the Christ.

Blow out the candles in any order you wish. As you do so, see the Light of the flame that is extinguished flowing into you, becoming part of you.

Give thanks for whatever blessings and insights you feel you have received.

Stand up and go about your daily business, in wholeness and grace, knowing that you can repeat this exercise at any time in the future that seems appropriate.

Chapter Seven:
Unveiling Christos

In this book, I have been focusing upon ways in which the Christ can be understood as a sacred function or activity within creation, a function/activity that is within us as well.

The overall intent, of course, is to assist us in experiencing the Christ as a presence within us—to unveil our inner Christos. One step in that direction, for me, is to make the idea of Christ and of being Christ more accessible. And one way to do that is to understand and realize the nature of Christ as a structural/incarnational activity within us.

This is not just a mental ploy or a philosophical idea. It comes from my actual visionary experience of the Christ and of our inner Christos.

As I said at the beginning, there are many Christologies and many ways of entering into a Christ experience. The one I am sharing here has been helpful to me, but it is not the only way by any means.

I have observed over the years that focusing on Christ as an activity which we share with the Sacred is a perspective that many people have found helpful and transformative. But it is only a first step, a beginning place. And it can lead to some confusion. The confusion lies in equating activity with role, role with identity, and identity with activity.

Let me explain.

A policeman is courageous and helps people. I can be courageous and helpful, too, but that doesn't make me a policeman. Likewise, the Christ is an activity of holding and expressing the "I", the sacredness at the root of each incarnation, and this activity, as I have described, can manifest as redemption (or re-alignment), incarnation, and the openness that comes from going to the edge of our boundaries. But does this mean that if I am redemptive, incarnated, and open, that I am also Christ? Does the activity create the identity or the role, or the other way around?

Let's reconsider the policeman. Many people, no matter what their roles or professions, can be courageous and helpful. Possession of those qualities and wanting to act in courageous and helpful ways can be what leads a person to become a policeman. These are not "police traits" per se but human qualities.

So, I could say that acting courageously and helpfully is not simply what makes me a policeman; it's what makes me more of a human being.

In some ways, we have come to think of Christ as a role in much the way that a policeman is a role. A policeman serves a function in society, but when I think of function, I'm thinking more of a natural law—a statement of how some aspect of creation functions—rather than a social role. Of course, engaging in a helpful activity is not by itself going to make me a policeman. But the function of helpfulness, the activity of helpfulness, goes beyond the role of policeman and is part of the deep structure of human nature that makes society possible. To create a society in the first place, people must act helpfully towards each other, at least to some extent. The capacity to act helpfully is structurally part of what it means to be human; it is a basic human function.

So, when I act helpfully, I am fulfilling part of my human potential. I am acting as a human being.

Before there is a courageous and helpful policeman, there is a courageous and helpful human being; before there is a courageous and helpful policeman, there is the structural human capacity to be helpful and courageous. When I am courageous and helpful, I am touching in to that deeper identity, whether I'm in the role of a policeman or not, or whether I have the skill, training, and other capacities to be a policeman or not.

By analogy, when I touch into activities and perform activities that resonate with the structure and function of Christ—with Christ as an activity within Cosmos—I am touching into and embodying that deeper identity, whether the outward appearance looks like "Christ" (in the historical or the miraculous sense) or not.

But then, is any activity that is "Christ-like" an embodiment of the Christ or is there more?

The practice known as "Imitatio Christi," or imitating Christ, is an ancient one with roots that go much farther back into shamanic and magical practices predating Christianity. The core of such a practice is, in effect, role playing, acting "as if." It is a practice that establishes a field of resonance through which a human individual can take on and manifest through mediation a much larger force, be it collective, planetary, cosmic, or sacred. By acting in a way that I think Christ would have acted, I come into resonance with the Christ Presence. In the words of a Catholic priest I once met, I "configure myself to Christ."

In this context, Christ is not an activity but a model for activities. And any activity that reflects that model can invoke the Christ Presence. My imitation of Christ can make Christ present in a situation, but I do not become Christ.

My perspective is different. We can certainly imitate Christ, and there is power and value in doing so. But for me, Christ is more than a model. Christ is an incarnational function that I also share. If I can discover that function in myself, then I don't just imitate Christ, I *am* Christ. Or more precisely, I am also an embodiment of that function I call Christ. This is a different thing altogether.

I can imitate a policeman in being helpful, but that

imitation will not make me a policeman. I can also understand that being helpful is not unique to a policeman, that it is a deeper function or activity within human consciousness. Therefore, when I am helpful, I am not imitating anybody. I am being myself, and what I am is a human being with a variety of capacities and functions that I can perform.

However, recognizing this and acting out of the identity of my capacities—the identity of my humanness—doesn't mean that I am expressing those capacities in the fullest way or the most mindful and conscious way, or in a way that empowers and enables others as well as myself to discover and embody their humanness in a fuller and deeper way. Using an activity to connect with my deeper identity is one thing; externalizing and expressing that identity more fully is something else.

So, just connecting Christ with certain (though not all) activities that we can and do perform is not a full expression of our Christic potential. Clearing my desk and experiencing it as a redemptive act can give me an "aha" sense of just who and what I am, the nature of Christ within me, and the nature of the sacred within me. But this is a beginning, not an ending. It shifts the playing field from always referencing Christ as something outside ourselves, transcendent to ourselves, or more miraculous (in the sense of creating miracles) than ourselves. It can put us in what I might call the lineage of Christ and gives a new insight into the idea of the Christ within us. Christ is not just a consciousness we put on; it is part of our very structure, part of the innate nature of our beingness.

The practice of "activitas Christi", the activity of Christ, or Christ as Activity, is more than just making a comparison. Clearing my desk is a redemptive, Christic activity (on a small scale) in my way of seeing things, but just saying so doesn't make it so. I must mindfully enter into that activity and make it a link with my sacredness, for that is what a Christ activity does. It doesn't redeem or clean or organize or realign just to be doing those things. It does these things as an offshoot of holding the presence of Sacredness immanently and accessibly within creation; it does these things to create a condition in which Sacredness is revealed and experienced in the midst of matter, activity, incarnation, and form—in the midst of cosmos. Christ is not a maid, though Christ activity may do maid-like things.

In the midst of my "redemptive" cleaning or clearing or reowning, I have to do the work of mind, heart, and spirit to make the sacramental link between this activity, its results, and my "I". What makes a "Christ-activity" Christ-filled—what unveils Christos—is that it fundamentally performs a sacred act of empowering and revealing sacredness: making the sacred more possible, more accessible, more active in the world.

The main ingredient of this process—though not the only one—is love. Love activates the sacramental relationship; it is the most fundamental and powerful act of magic in creation. And along with love comes will, the will to hold life, matter, and incarnation in a sacred and empowering way.

At the risk of oversimplifying and repetition, let me again use the example of cleaning my desk as a redemptive activity. The reason is not that Christ likes to tidy up creation or fixes messes or is a cosmic housecleaner per se. The Christ acts to keep a clear channel open to the Sacred within all the activity of creation so that the "dust" raised by that activity, so to speak, doesn't clog the channel. The Christ upholds all that enables the clear and clean circulation of consciousness between the Unmanifest and the Manifest, the universal and the particular, or the sacred and the ordinary, however you might wish to put it.

Why do I clean my desk? Because the clutter that has accumulated is clogging up my flow. As a creative space, my desk is obstructed. It has ceased to BE a creative space.

Now I can go at this job from a frame of mind that says, "Let me get rid of this clutter. Let me fix this desk!" But that is not how Christ goes at it. Remember, Christ is not a "cleaning-up" activity per se but a "creating conditions for flow and alignment so that God can be fully manifested" activity. So, the Christic aspect of this desk-cleaning activity is one that doesn't name things as "junk" and "clutter" nor sees the surface of the desk as needing to be "fixed." Rather it identifies each piece as part of cosmos and seeks to find the right place for it so that balance and flow are restored (note that the right place might be in the waste basket!). It acts in a mindful, intelligent, willing, and loving way.

Can I do the same? Can I discover the Christ activity in the activity of cleaning my desk? Yes, I feel I can, but it takes mindfulness, it takes recognition that I am this Christ activity and that I'm not simply imitating anyone, it takes love and caring, and it takes willingness to deepen into the sacramental and Christic aspect of the activity, acknowledging both my own sacredness and the sacred within the desk and the things that are on it.

When I become aware that there are activities and functions in me, capacities that are woven into my being, that are not simply Christ-like but are actually Christic in nature, I take a step towards unveiling and expression my inner Christos. Christianity for the most part either restricts such a realization exclusively to Jesus—only Jesus is the Christ—or views Christhood as a special state, achievable only through extraordinary spiritual and psychological effort.

As you are probably gathering by now from this book,

I do not see Christ or Christhood as a special state per se. It is an expression of the sacred function that incarnates sacredness into form (not necessarily physical form), holds that incarnation so that its sacredness is co-creatively accessible and available to the rest of creation, and thus unites the Unmanifest and Manifest realms in a totality, much as Light is the totality uniting a particle and a wave. As such, it is a fundamental activity within creation and one that is entirely natural and organic. To be a Christ is a very natural thing (which appears unnatural, extraordinary, and special to us because our minds are clouded to a sense of what is truly natural to a human being—or to life as a whole).

However, there are thresholds. I can be courageous and helpful in my everyday life, but a policeman or fireman takes these same qualities—which are human qualities—and intensifies them, embodies them more consciously and deliberately, and quickens and heightens them to where they become an expression not only of activity but of identity as well. I do not expect to go into harm's way for others as a daily occurrence, but a policeman or fireman does. It is what they do. They have crossed a threshold of courage and helpfulness that the ordinary citizen does not and need not cross except in extraordinary circumstances.

In an analogous way, there are thresholds with Christ-ness as well. There are those beings in whom the beingness and doingness of Christic activity crosses a threshold and becomes their identity. They are carriers of the Christ Presence, the Christ Consciousness, or the Christ Principle. They "do" Christness as a daily matter, so to speak.

When I meet a policeman or a fireman, I recognize and honor their commitment to being courageous and helpful as a profession, and I am inspired by their example to reflect upon, discover, and honor my own courage and helpfulness.

I may not have to go into harm's way and put my life on the line, but I can be inspired to give greater expression to the activities of courage and helpfulness as they manifest in my own circumstances. I do not become "policeman-like" to do so, nor do I need to mimic what a policeman does. Courage and helpfulness are human traits that both the policeman and I share, as I have said, and we can inspire them in each other.

So, when I meet a being who is what I might colloquially call a Christ—a being who is embodying and doing the activity and function of Christos in a "professional" way—I can be uplifted, quickened, inspired, energized, blessed by such a presence. I can honor and revere that presence, just as I would honor and revere a policeman, AND I can recognize that what it is, I am, too. We share the same nature and the same activities, even though that being or person is operating at another level of intensity and mindfulness with those activities than I am.

There is another distinction that I'd like to make here as well. I distinguish between a Christ and an Avatar. Jesus to my mind was both. The traditional definition of an avatar is that it is a divine incarnation or the deliberate and focused incarnation of one or more particular divine qualities. I might say that an avatar is the manifestation of a sacred idea made flesh. Avatars appear for different reasons, but one reason is to be an exemplar and a demonstration.

Christ—that is to say, the nature and importance of what Christ is as a universal function that is part of our collective and individual sacred natures—is a divine idea. Christ is an idea in the mind of God. God conceived and imagined the activity/function/presence that is Christ before it became manifest. Thus, there can be avataric manifestations of the pure idea of Christ, demonstrators and exemplars of what Christ is.

Such beings go beyond just embodying Christness in the moment and embody something else, perhaps the sacred presence that gave birth to Christness. Their presence enables Christos, kindling it, empowering it, fostering it in the worlds and realms where their influence operates.

To some extent, anyone who awakens to Christos within themselves, as we seek to do in this book by focusing upon simple, ordinary activities that nonetheless have a Christic resonance, will inspire the expression of Christos. Any awakening to the sacred enables all further and subsequent awakenings to some degree. But the avatar function is specifically one that has awakening and deepening as its "professional" objective. And an avatar is always a gift.

To me, whatever else he was, Jesus was such an avatar or became part of and anchored into our world a Christic avatar event…one which, as I said at the very beginning of our book, is still continuing and of which we are all a part.

As you see, there are many ways we can encounter Christos, but the most important thing is to awaken the realization that we ARE Christos and to begin the process of deepening and embodying that realization so that it becomes our living presence.

Then we become Christos unveiled.

THE PUBLISHER

Lorian Press LLC is a private, for profit business which publishes works approved by the Lorian Association. Current titles can be found here https://lorianpress.etsy.com

The Lorian Association is a not-for-profit educational organization. Its work is to help people bring the joy, healing, and blessing of their personal spirituality into their everyday lives. This spirituality unfolds out of their unique lives and relationships to Spirit, by whatever name or in whatever form that Spirit is recognized. For more information, go to www.lorian.org.

www.ingramcontent.com/pod-product-compliance
Lightning Source LLC
Chambersburg PA
CBHW040054100426
42734CB00043B/3267